DOG
EMERGENCIES
What to do in a Pet Emergency

Everything Dogs Book Collection, Mercy Lopez

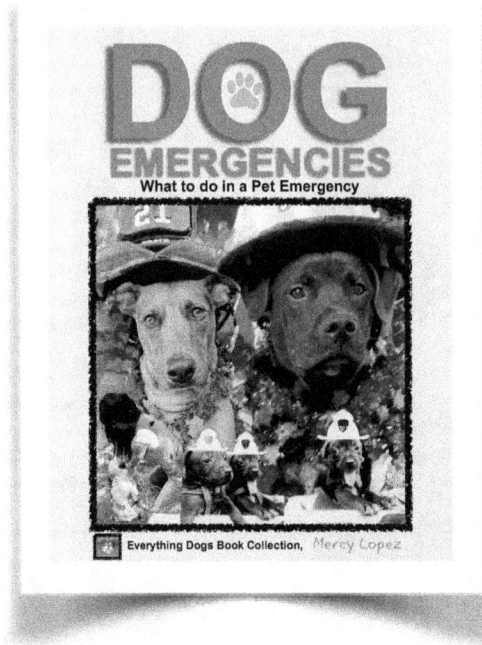

Dog Emergencies
What to do in a Pet Emergency
Everything Dogs Series Collection
Dog Education

By Mercy Lopez

Book design, and published by:
photo-video journalist, author, educator. animal advocate, activist, actress, model, stunt woman, and songwriter

Mercy Lopez

www.everythingdogs.net

ISBN 978-0-9980415-7-5

About the Author

is a first generation Cuban/Spanish American, photojournalist, animal advocate, media influencer, foster mom, volunteer, dog rehabilitator, book author, educator and is also a vegan. What is really interesting about her animal adoption photography and video productions, aside from the fact that she really captures dogs real personality off

the dogs, is that she uses her original music in them.

Mercy's background in music as a guitarist/song writer developed in being a ASCAP (American Society of Composers) member and a recording artist with BMG Germany out of Berlin for 3 years.

"Show me" Video!

Binky & Sabien, "No Idea" Sunset Music Video!

The Mercy Lopez Band Live Video!

4

Mercy is pictured here on the right as a blonde, onset filming of a Toyota, Prius commercial in the 90s as a blond at South Beach!

She is originally from Miami, then South Beach, where she won a Harley Davidson in a beauty contest sponsored by Cristal Aguardiente and Venus Swimwear 1992. This led Mercy into modeling on the pages of Playboy, (as a blonde and a brunette), numerous videos, commercial work, BMG Germany recording artist, acting in soap operas in the Mexico DF with TV Azteca, as well as SAG acting jobs with: Oliver Stone's in *"On Any Givin Sunday"*; The Farrelly Brothers' in *"Something About Mary"*; Adam Sandler's in *"Water Boy"*; and Micheal Bays' in *"Bad Boy II" (as a* SAG/stunt action woman). Working in these industries gave Mercy a good understanding of working with lighting and composition for her own photography and video productions.

Mercy then sold her investment property, in Little Havana, Florida to relocated to West Palm Beach, Florida, where she practiced as a commodities broker and a Realtor. She jogged and walked her dogs twice everyday, found lots of dogs and develop a reputation as "The Dog Lady" in the neighborhood. By her coming across so many stray dogs, it led her to help dogs out many ways like volunteering and fostering at the local shelters and rescues. At one point (for a few years), she went every Sunday to her community shelter till closing. She even got locked in the kennel adoption floor a lot, because it was hard for her to leave. Helping dogs keeps Mercedes/Mercy very busy and it is especially rewarding to her when, she see's the faces of rescued pets together with their new forever family.

With the great support she received from social media and happy adoptions, it encouraged Mercy to spend about 5 years of her extra time, into getting her new book collection just right to publish. It has more detail than, she has in her previously published 15 mini iBooks. It's everything she thinks that's important for every dog guardian or animal lover.

She admits that volunteering can be challenging work that, has left her with some very unsettling experiences. This is why writing these books brought Mercy lots of healing by honoring so many dogs she

worked with and their memories here. It is apparent that, every dog she has worked with has deeply touched her heart.

Mercy says, "It's very important to attract attention by generating media interest in animal issues like sterilization programs, dog training, assisting animals in our communities, finding successful homes and most importantly, to reduce animal intake and euthanasia in shelters everywhere". With photography, video and social media, she knows that we can reach the masses, for successful adoptions and sterilization. She sees positive improvements every year!

It is very apparent on Mercy's Facebook page, that her passion burns deep with enthusiasm and she is full of positive optimism.

She hopes that her work encourages you to help out animals in some way.

Just click on the blue links to check out some of her videos and get to know her awesome furry friends!

Avery's Adoption Video **and** Hannah's Adoption Video**!**

CBS "Pet of the Day" with Avery & Hannah

Facebook Live, CBS Channel 12's Pet of the Day!

Mercy's Portfolio Pictures

Mercy's Portfolio Pictures

On the previous page from left to right, going down:

- With Oliver Stone, on set filming "On Any Given Sunday"
- With Henry Winkler and Adam Sandler on set filming "Water Boy"
- Mercedes as Black Widow series model for Marble, Wizard and Max Comic Books, by Greg Horn.
- With LL Cool Jay on "Any Given Sunday".
- With Lenny Kravitz
- Germany BMG "Show Me" music video.
- Mercy Lopez Band performing in Berlin
- Black Widow Cover
- Toyota Prius Commercial with a pink dog
- "Universal Soldier" with Jean-Claude Van Dam.
- Guitarist for Luis Enrique, Universal music
- Playboy September 1992's, "Girls of South Beach"
- With Mr. Olympia Bob Paris. Catalog work in Cancun, Mexico
- Pepsi

Mercy's Foster Stella

Stella's Story Video

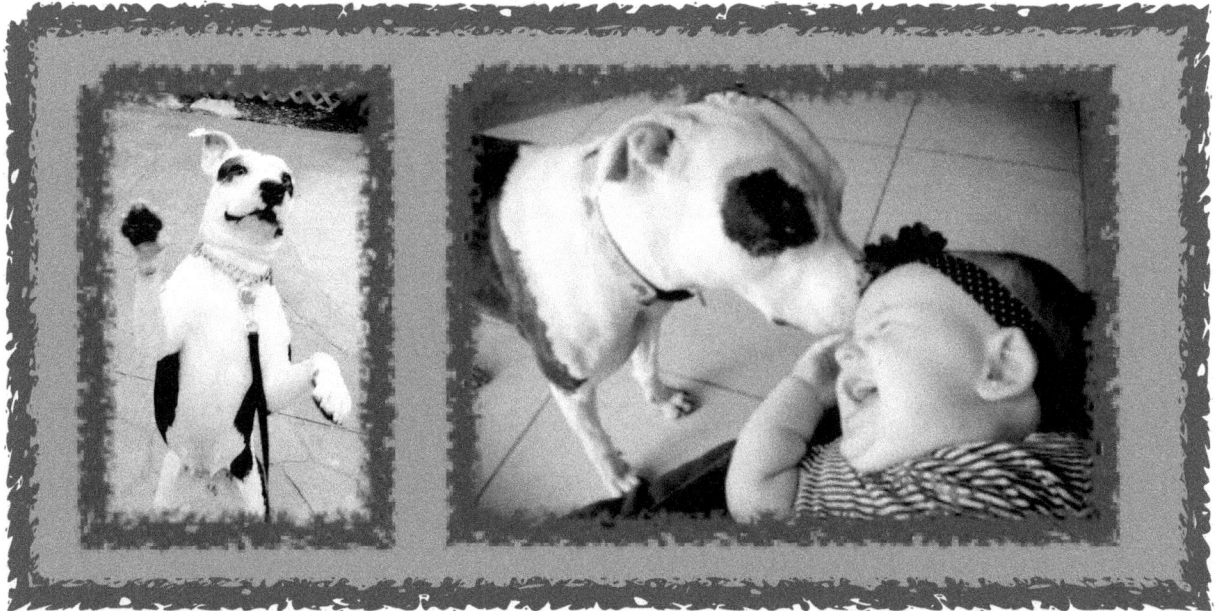

Mercy's Singing Dogs Here!

Introduction
Everything Dogs Book Collection

<u>Everything Dogs Series Introduction Video</u>

<u>Everything Dogs 15 minutes Mini Movie Here!</u>

Everything Dogs Collection Book Project is based on true shelter dog photography and video stories (with original music from the author-publisher), combined with detailed research of everything pet guardians and animal lovers should know about dogs.

Everything Dog's was designed to: enhance our relationship with dogs, reduce animal intake, assist eliminate euthanasia numbers in shelters, educate on today's animal overpopulation situation in shelters in the United State's, encourage: fostering, volunteering, sterilization, adopting, basic dog training and humane holistic health maintenance animal care, even during a pet emergency.

All of the collections books contain many pet guardians tips that, can lead to an enhanced, positive, safe and loving relationship with your furry family member.

Proceeds of Everything Dogs Education Book Collection go to animal rescue charity partners.

Here is more information on what this book **"Dog's Emergencies - What to do in a Pet Emergency". First of all, it is a quick training manual to prepare you in case of a rescue emergency with your pet or any dog that may need your fast action assistance covers in detail:**

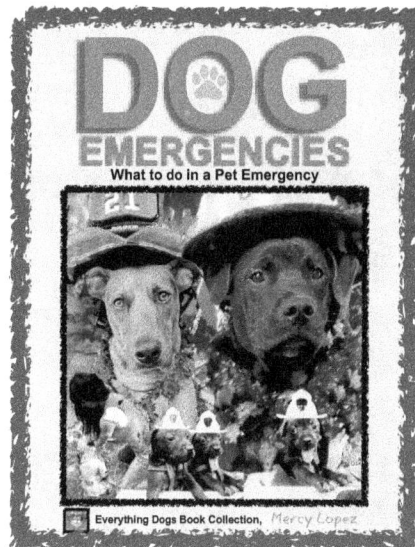

Most Common Pet Emergencies, How to Respond, Rescue Protocols, First Aid, What to do if your dog is Over-Heating, How to Perform Heimlich maneuver if your dog is choking, CPR/ Cardiopulmonary Resuscitation on your pet, Safety demonstration videos and more!

Other Everything Dogs Book Collections includes:
• *"Operation Saving Shelter Dogs - True Shelter Dog Stories and Everything You Should Know"* goes over in detail:

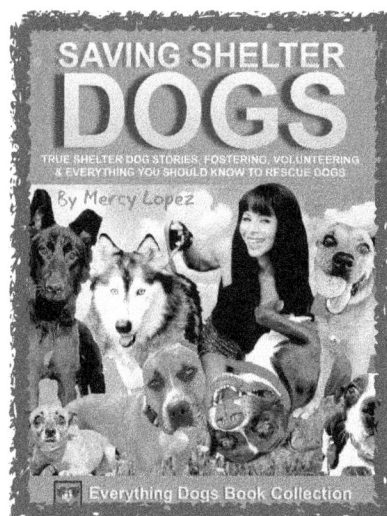

The Truth About Animal Shelters, True Shelter Dog Stories (with videos and full-color pictures stories), Statistics, Fostering, Volunteering, Anti-Tethering Law, Condition of Intake Dogs, Common Choking Collar Accidents, Lost, Stray and Found Animals, What We are Doing to Bring our Animal Intake and Euthanasia Numbers Down, Sterilization, Euthanasia, High-Risk Animals, Black Dog Syndrome, Kennel-Mates Save Lives, Foster Dog Stories, Playgroup-Playing for Life Program, Count Down to Zero Initiative Program, Pitbull History, Breed Specific Legislation (BSL), How we are Saving Lives in our Communities and more!

- **Getting Started on the Right Paw - Basic Dog Training - Introducing Your New Dog to Your Home, Other Pets and more!** Includes:

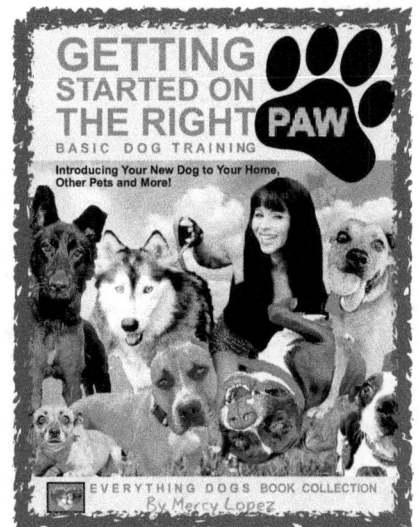

How to Pick the Right Pet Together as a Family, Statistics, What to Consider When Adopting a Dog, True Shelter Dog's Pictures and Video Stories Links, Children and Dogs, How to Introduce Your New Dog to Your Home and

Other Exciting Pets, How to Doggie Proof Your Home and Yard, How To Get Ready for Your New Dog to Come Home, Safety, House Training, Chewing, Leaving Pets Home Alone, How to Avoid Bathroom Accidents, Basic Dog Training, Placement, Rewards for Your Dogs, Basic Commands, Leash Pulling, Heel and more!

•Dogs Holistic Health Maintenance and Remedies Encyclopedia:

This book goes over the details of: Dog Holistic Healing, Natural Alternatives, Essential Oils, Herbs, Natural Repellents, Different Skin Conditions, Hot Spots, Yeast, Staff Infection, Demodex, Natural Holistic Fleas and Ticks, Prevention and Natural Alternatives, Ears, Eyes, Teeth, Gums, Older Dog's Health, Super Healing Roots, Super-Greens Supplementation, Benefits of Basic Herbs, Herbal Tonic Remedies, Vaccines, Holistic Alternatives and Remedies, Heartworms, Natural Prevention for Flea, Tick, Heartworm and Mosquitos for your Lawn and Home, Homeopathic Do It Yourself

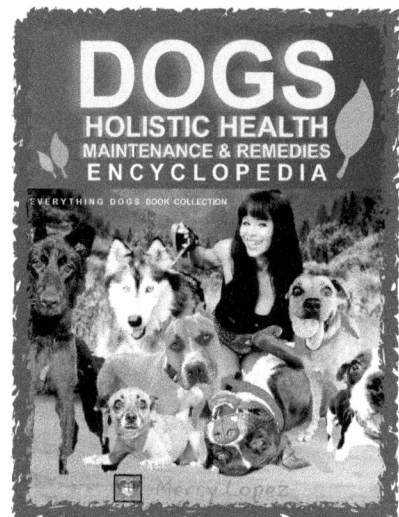

Sprays, Vaccines, Medications, Foods You Can and Can Not Feed Your Dogs, Gluten-Free Grains, Prebiotic, Probiotics, Live Enzymes, Leaky Gut, Basic Nutrition Your Dog Needs on a Vegan Diet, Dog Health Maintenance and Holistic Natural Alternative Remedies, pH Balance, What is in Your Pet's Food, Nutrition, Vegan Food Full Color Pictures, and Recipes.

I hope that you will look at animal overpopulation in your own back yard, differently, and compassionately.

After volunteering at shelters, I am more aware of the truth that, takes place in animal shelters. I just wanted to share with you a little bit of what the dogs are like, based on my experience, their story and dedicate this to all the souls of animals that never walk out of a shelter alive. After collecting tremendous amounts of someone like you, to save a dog or help. No animal's life should end shortly because, they don't have a home or space in the shelter.

Warning: This inspiring education book may cause a sudden urge to start saving dog's lives. You might even end up being a possible foster failure!

Open your heart to fostering, volunteering, donating and adopting. All animals can enhance your life, bring your happiness and even benefit your health!

Special Dedication to Binky

On June 1, 2011, I was walking my dogs before heading to a yoga class. My neighbor approached me with this beautiful black and white, female, Pitbull mix dog. He had just found her in the vacant lot next to us. He gave her to me because, he knew I was a dog person and saw me walking my two dogs every day, twice a day. I named her "Binky". She was about a year old, so cute, sweet and beautiful that, I could not resist, to immediately help her out. I brought her home, gave her food, water and took care of her, until I could hopefully get her back to her owners. I got her immediately scanned for a mi-

crochip, but she did not have one, or any identification tag. I followed the legal protocol for lost and found dogs. I thought someone must be missing and/or looking for her because of the red collar she had on, so followed found dog protocol. I quickly starting to put up lost/found dog flyers and signs everywhere, so she would be visible for her family to find her. I took advantage of all the free ads in the major local newspapers. I also posted her picture on the Palm Beach County Animal Care and Control website page; under found dog like you are supposed to do, so that lost dogs can be reunited.

For days, we covered the entire area for miles to find her family, but no one had seen her before or knew who she belonged to, During this time, she became part of my pack of dogs and we fell in love with her.

After 10 days, I received a call from Animal Care and Control telling me to bring Binky in that, I can adopt her by putting a "reserve adoption hold" so I could take her back home with me.

When I brought her to Animal Care and Control, they asked me to wait for her while they checked her out privately. When they came back out, I was handed Binky's new collar and leash. I was told that Binky had to be put on a 10-day hold at the shelter to allow her legal guardian the opportunity to find her and start the 10 day process again. I was heartbroken. I was even more confused when, they told me that, I could not see or visit her while she was there. I thought How is her family going to find her? This was a very difficult realization. While I was there I observed how our community "kill shelters" are understaffed and under-budgeted. This, in turn, lacks to provide animals the attention, space, care they need and deserve.

City commissioners set out budgets for county departments and the last departments they consider

funding are the ones that don't have a voice; like the animal service divisions known as animal control shelters in our community.

Finally, Binky's 10 days of being locked up in an unfamiliar scary kennel were over. I returned to Palm Beach County Animal Care and Control to rush my adoption application through; to get my "Stinky Binky" out. They told me again that, I could not see her and I would have to wait for an inspector to come out to my property (this took another 2 weeks). Finally, the inspection was complete. At this point, she was ready for surgery to get spayed/sterilized for final adoption with me. After her surgery, I still could not see or take her home. Apparently, she was bleeding internally, due to a towel she ate that, she was still passing. I believe she eat the towel out of boredom, mind deteriorating and by not getting the attention she mentally and physically needed in a

confined kennel space for such a long time. During this time, she developed Canine Infectious Respiratory Disease (CIRD), also known as Kennel Cough or a doggie cold. It's very similar to a human cold and very common. If she had the Bordatella vaccination given by her previous owner veterinarian, it would have prevented her from getting sick. Her time was running out at the shelter, when, I finally got a call saying that, "if you want her, then come get her now!".

Of course, I rushed to pick her up! On June 21, 2011, she officially became a member of our family. This was the longest month of my life. Aside from what she went through, her dramatic experience of being separated from me like that, but also she was taking up unnecessary space in a kill shelter that, could have kept some dogs alive.

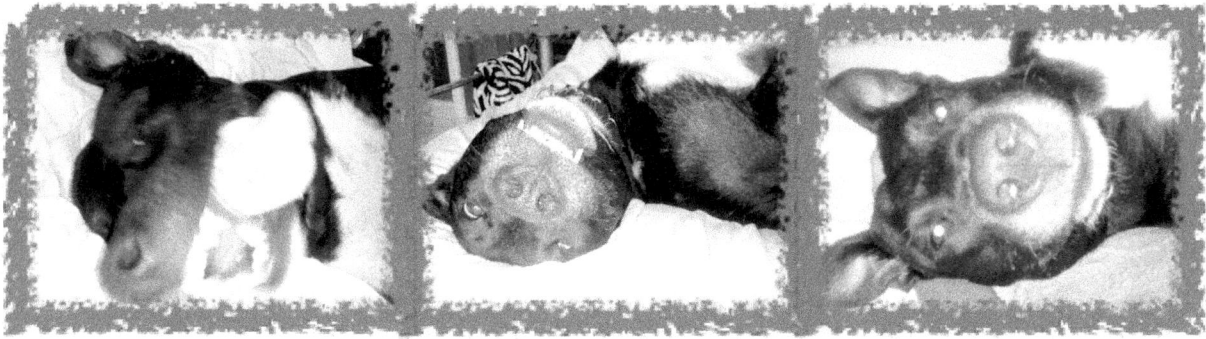

Everything Dogs Series Introduction Video

Check out a video clip of when Binky was given back to me and the special magical connection we had. How she recognized me and how we felt about one another. She was so excited and happy.

Through volunteering at a shelter, I later became friends with that same staff member who gave Binky back to me. She said she remembered that moment because, she had never seen a dog be so happy being pick up like that before; showing so much love to a stranger. Not knowing that, I had her with me for a short while and brought her in.

Soon after this experience, I decided to look into how I could help animals in my community at this particular kill shelter, even though I had volunteered at other local animal rescue organizations. The more I saw, the more I realized that I had to somehow do more! Binky opened my eyes to how animals suffer in shelters because, of the current system in place and lack of sterilization. People say it is difficult to help out, so they just don't help out at all. We can change this attitude by showing in these books that, there are many different ways to help animals in dire need in your area. By giving a little bit of your time, love and affection to a shelter, or rescue organizations we can turn this awful animal overpopulation situation into a more positive one.

Binky was four years old when in the middle of the night she mysteriously started coughing up blood. The morning before she went for a jog alongside me as, I rollerbladed up the street, of course, I immediately rushed to get her the best help that, I could. I was scheduled to filming CBS - Channel 12's "Pet of the Day" that next morning. I was faced with having to drop my Binky off at the veterinarian to run some tests and be separated from her for the first time since, our animal control experience. She had veterinarian check-up's a month before, showing that she was healthy. They gave a Heartworm preventative treatment injection for her first time. With this being said, I could not imagine anything being wrong with her but wondered if the heartworm pre-vention shot had something to do with this.

I took Binky to 4 different veterinarian specialist and we gave her every test that could help her available. No test or doctor could explain to us why her lungs were filling up so fast! They took out a minimum of 850 cc's of bloody fluid from her lungs each time (above pictures). She needed five emergency surg-eries to drain the blood out of her lungs. She also had two blood transfusions from "Apollo" from GTS Husky Rescue; shown here.

Apollo and I on "CBS Pet of the Day" Video!

During the course of the next ten days of her suffering, Binky could no longer lay down. It was as if she was drowning and suffocating from the blood filling up in her lungs. We could not sleep at all from holding her up so that, she could get some relief and rest while sleeping sitting up. Her lungs con-tinued to refill faster every day with

more blood, every breath for her was a struggle. You could hear the liquid build-up gurgling in her lungs. It was devastating for our family. Dr. Martin from Jupiter Animal Health Clinic worked with her end-lessly, hoping that we could find out what was wrong with her to save her.

Some of the tests available would take two weeks for the results to get back to us. Time Binky didn't have. We treated her with vitamin K, thinking maybe she ate some poison and with "Yunnan Baiyao" (a hard to find Chinese herb, used during the Vietnam war to help stop bleeding). It changed the color of the fluid in her lungs, as you can see in the pictures shown above.

We did our best to figure out the mystery of why her lungs were disintegrating like gel. It was killing her! During this time, I learned that the veterinary field

had its limitation. This may have been beneficial for my Binky at the time.

On November 21, 2014, Binky went into her last emergency surgery. Her last specialist veterinarian had installed tubes with knobs on each side of her, into her lungs in desperate measures to save her. This was so that, I could drain out the excess fluids in her lungs and help her breath. Her lungs kept on filling up with more bloody fluid, faster each day. We knew it was a very dangerous and sensitive proce-dure, but we thought this could help buy more time while we find out what was wrong and how to treat her. She needed medical intervention. We were run-ning out of options for fighting off blood infections and transfusion risks. Her doctor said that she tried to take 2 breaths and died coming out of the anes-thesia from surgery. I had a few moments with her and saw all the knobs and tubes sticking out of her in the attempt to save her. I never saw a dog fight so hard to live! I have never done so much in an attempt to keep a dog alive in such a short period of time.

After the necropsy, which is an autopsy for dogs, the doctor's opinion of the cause of death was idiopathic, meaning "unexplainable". They found that the blood clots and infection from the blood in her lungs was conclusive with what were going on with her. I still have no explanation as to what happened to my Binky. We could not find out why her lungs reacted this way. Maybe if there was more research, Binky would have lived a long life. I wish that we could have at least know what happened that, caused her lungs to disintegrate into a gel.

The mystery of what happened to my Binky still haunts me and remains in my memory. This experience still haunts me!

Because of what I have learned about the overall mentality of our government that mandates excessive vaccines, the animal maintenance care industry (controlled by animal pharmaceuticals, plus large pet

foods corporations preservatives in packaged foods) is possibly poisoning our pets. I believe that there are links to why so many dogs are commonly getting cancer at alarming numbers.

I know that there is a great deal of room for research and improvements for the advancement of veterinary medicine. I had another dog; "Ralph", that also had issues with lung cancer; as well as my "Joy Bird", that died of cancer. One of my dogs, "Hawk-eye", died from eating a commercially sold rawhide. Manufactures knows rawhide commonly kills dogs and they continue to sell them! I'm thinking, "Could some of this be relevant to the pet foods that we feed our pets? Maybe there is a link with vaccines? Do you wonder too?

I now look at everything pertaining to dogs' health differently since, my experience with Binky. I question the dog health industries, the consumer products that are made available and advertised in today's modern convenient package food industry. So, I did extensive research for my own dogs' health and maintenance so that I can bring to you *the Dogs Holistic Health Maintenance and Remedies En-*

cyclopedia" book. I highly recommend for: health wellness conscious animal lover friends, .

Binky's passing away inspired me in many ways. Aside from helping at dog shelters and I also took a "foster challenge". I fostered five dogs in honor of the five surgical attempts to try to save Binky. As of now, I have surpassed that goal and have found many pets awesome safe homes. I now hope to raise money and to promote animal awareness with Everything Dogs Book Collection Project to help families and pooches!

My last picture with my "Binky" (bottom right) after her 4th surgery attempt trying to save her.

Binky Rounding Up Chickens!

Sabien & Binky Singing Together!

Ralph & Rodger

Love you & always in my heart. RIP.

I've had other dogs than Binky that had suffered from lung cancer and wonder why it is so common for dogs if they don't smoke. Could it be linked to the food that is sold to us commercially that is loaded with toxic preservatives, the additives, synthetic ingredient for the manufacture to meet the standard of nutrition to be sold to us because they are cooked at such high temperature that it kills the nutrition and that cause harm?

Special Thanks

I want to thank my: Binky, Sabien, Hawkeye, Joy Bird, Mac, Ralph, Blankie, Benji, Broggie, Harley and Davidson. As well as my foster failures: Juno, Pretzel, Rodger, Mindy, and Coco for continuing to inspire me. They filled my heart with love.

I wish everyone could experience as many awesome memories with their furry family members too!

Thank you for taking the time to invest in your dogs and for your interest in the world of Everything Dogs!

Kim Tunney Johnson

I want to give recognition to this very talented, speedy, co-proofing editor. She is very sharp in the field of being a paralegal and is always multi-tasking. She has full custody of her adopted, sweet, beautiful granddaughter "Karina". She used to have more time to foster urgent status dogs and help out at the shelter. She helped save "Hope", a blind dog's life, that is now happily re-homed. Kim was a victim of her own dog being stolen by a burglar from home. She has never fully recovered from the loss of her furry loved one. She is an animal activist and is always helping out dogs; in the best ways that she can.

Disclaimer

Everything Dogs Book Collection is based on true rescue dog stories. It is intended for public education, to help families develop a lasting and healthy relationship with their pets. I feel if people can implement some of the information in these books, we can compassionately bring our animal intake and euthanasia numbers down in high kill shelters.

The publisher and author are not responsible for any specific health, or any allergy needs that may require medical supervision and not liable for any damages, or negative consequences from any treatments, actions, applications or preparations to any pet or person in regards to the reading or following any of the information contained in this book.

For diagnosis or treatment of any medical situation, always consult your professional veterinarian immediately.

Neither the publisher nor the individual author shall be liable for any physical, psychological, emotional, financial or commercial damages. Including, but not limited to: special, incidental, consequential or other damages. You are responsible for your own choices, actions, decisions, and results.

References are provided for informational purposes only and do not constitute an endorsement of any websites or other sources.

Readers should be aware that the web links listed in this book may change. No warranties or guarantees are expressed or implied by the publisher's choice to include any of the content in this book.

Table of Contents

Chapter 1

Travel First Aid Kit

In case of an emergency with your dog or someone else's dog, being prepared and ready to access your first aid kit, followed by quick thinking is necessary to handle the situation. This is going to be a very important factor in saving a dog's life.

Keep your pet's first aid kit in your car and take it with you when traveling. To start your first aid kit, you can buy a first-aid kit designed for people and add pet-specific items to it. You can also purchase a pet

Tonka

first-aid kit from a pet supply store or catalog. You can easily assemble your kit by gathering items like these:

• Dog leash, water, disinfectant, cotton balls, gauze tape, scissors, which will assist you if you come across any injured dog and/or cat.

• Blankets and towels can be used to lay over the dog or cat, to create protection and safety for the animal and you. It's a great asset for moving the injured animal, as well as transport to an emergency clinic.

• Phone numbers to your veterinarian, or the nearest emergency veterinary clinic are a must. Always be prepared!

• Pet's Medical records should be stored in a waterproof container or bag. Proof of rabies vaccination status, copies of other important medical records and a current photo of your pet in case they are lost. Please ensure all animals are microchipped for scanning identification that reads your current information correctly. Also, testing it to ensure your information pulls up correctly, with a backup number to a relative or close friend. If you have changed your phone number or moved from your registered address, make sure you update it within a month.

•Muzzle or strips of cloth to prevent biting (don't use this if the animal is vomiting because it can cause choking).

•Self-cling bandage (this will not stick to fur)

Home First Aid Kit

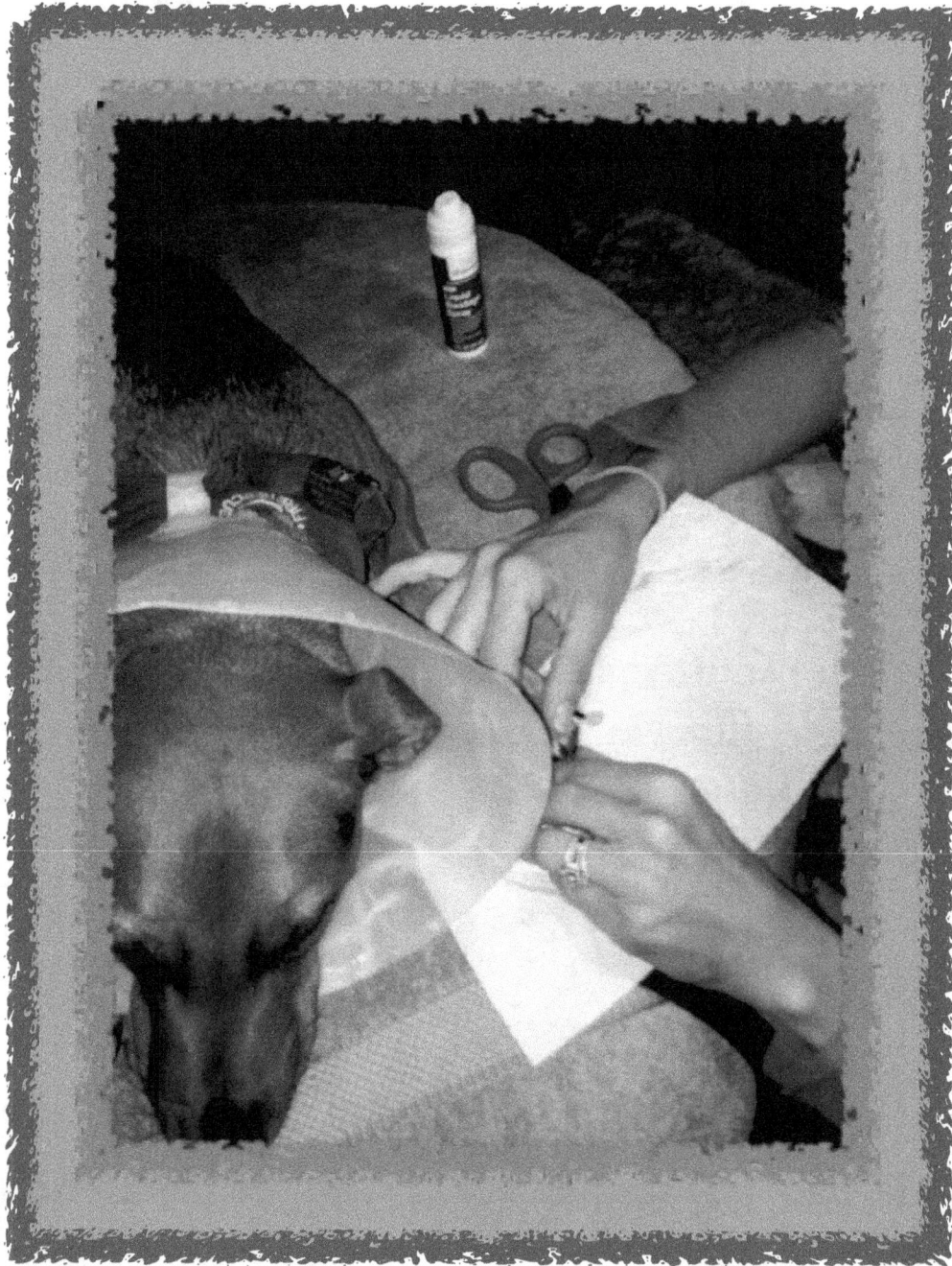

Absorbent gauze pads, adhesive tape, antiseptic wipes, lotion, powder or spray, cotton balls or swabs, gauze rolls, hydrogen peroxide (to induce vomiting, only do this only when directed by a veterinarian or a poison-control expert), ice pack, non-latex disposable gloves, petroleum jelly (to lubricate the thermometer), rectal thermometer (your pet's temperature should not rise above 103°F or fall below 100°F), scissors (with blunt ends), sterile non-stick gauze pads for bandages, sterile saline solution (sold at pharmacies), tweezers, pet collar guard (as shown on picture above), and a pet carrier.

Other useful items: Diphenhydramine (Benadryl®), is an antihistamine. That means it is typically used for allergic reactions. If approved by a veterinarian for allergic reactions. A veterinarian must tell you the correct dosage for your pet's size. The standard dosage for oral Benadryl is 1 mg per pound of bodyweight, given 2-3 times a day. Most drug store diphenhydramine tablets are 25 mg, which is the size used for a 25-pound dog. Always double-check the dosage before giving an over the counter medication. Also, many formulations are combined with other medications, such as Tylenol, so make sure Benadryl tablets contain only diphenhydramine.

Also include ear-cleaning solution, glucose paste or corn syrup (for diabetic dogs or those with low blood sugar), nail clippers, non-prescription antibiotic ointment, penlight or flashlight, plastic eye dropper or syringe, rubbing alcohol (isopropyl) to clean the thermometer, splints and depressors, styptic powder or pencil (sold at veterinary hospitals, pet-supply stores, and your local pharmacy), needle-nosed pliers, and tweezers. While this seems like a huge list, consider what you'd purchase for your child. A pet is essentially like a child. You must provide the necessities to make their lives happy.

Check the supplies in your pet's first-aid kit occasionally and replace any items that have expired or been used.

For your family's safety, keep all medical supplies and medications out of the reach of children and pets. Reaction to a drug prescribed for humans is the most common cause of poisoning in dogs. Ingredients such as acetaminophen or ibuprofen are pain relievers and cold medicine, and they can be deadly for your dog!

First Aid for Trauma

Trauma cases we see include roadside traffic accidents, falls, bites, damaged limbs and gunshot wounds. It can be difficult to assess the severity of internal trauma and you are urged to take the animal to receive proper veterinary care immediately. Some injuries, such as a ruptured lung or internal bleeding can take time to show, but they can be life-threatening. Wounds can be deeper than they appear and complications such as infection can develop if veterinary treatment is delayed. Most of these sorts of trauma cause a great deal of pain. Therefore, the animal will benefit from a pain-killing injection.

• If a joint or paw is bruised and swollen, do not follow these guidelines, there may be deeper injuries and you should consult your local vet immediately.

• If the wound is dirty, clean with warm salt water (1 teaspoon of salt in 1 pint of water). Use a soft cloth or towel to clean the injury. Avoid cotton, wool and other loose-fibered materials, as the threads often stick to the wound.

- Apply a cold compress, such as a bag of frozen vegetables or a cold, wet towel. Keep it in place for a few minutes.

- Bandage the wound to keep the dog from licking it.

- Call your vet for further advice, describing the injury and, if you know what caused it.

- Keep some emergency liquid glue for cuts. You must make sure it is disinfected inside the wound. Apply product while the cut is fresh for it to properly close.

- Bandages need to be changed every day until the wound heals and you should ensure the bandage remains dry. If you notice any purulent (puss-like) discharge, swelling, redness of the wound or an unpleasant smell coming from the bandages when you change them, contact your vet immediately.

First Aid for Dog Seizures

First of all, protect your dog, and yourself by making sure furniture, stairs, steps and sharp objects are out of the way to keep your pet safe. Protect yourself because some dogs may become aggressive when having a seizure. You need to know that your dog is not in control during a seizure. Countless humans have been injured by trying to keep their dog from swallowing their tongue, often resulting in a severe bite. Dogs do not swallow their tongues.

Seizures raise a dog's temperature and it's helpful to gently sponge the dog with lukewarm water on the tummy, armpit area, and head to help bring the temperature down. Use caution when doing this. An ice pack placed on the dog's back, right next to the neck, may shorten the dog's seizure while helping to bring the dog's temperature down.

Watch the clock and pay attention to the time. The longer the seizure, the more damage it may cause to your pet. You should consult with your vet or an emergency clinic if it lasts more than 5 minutes.

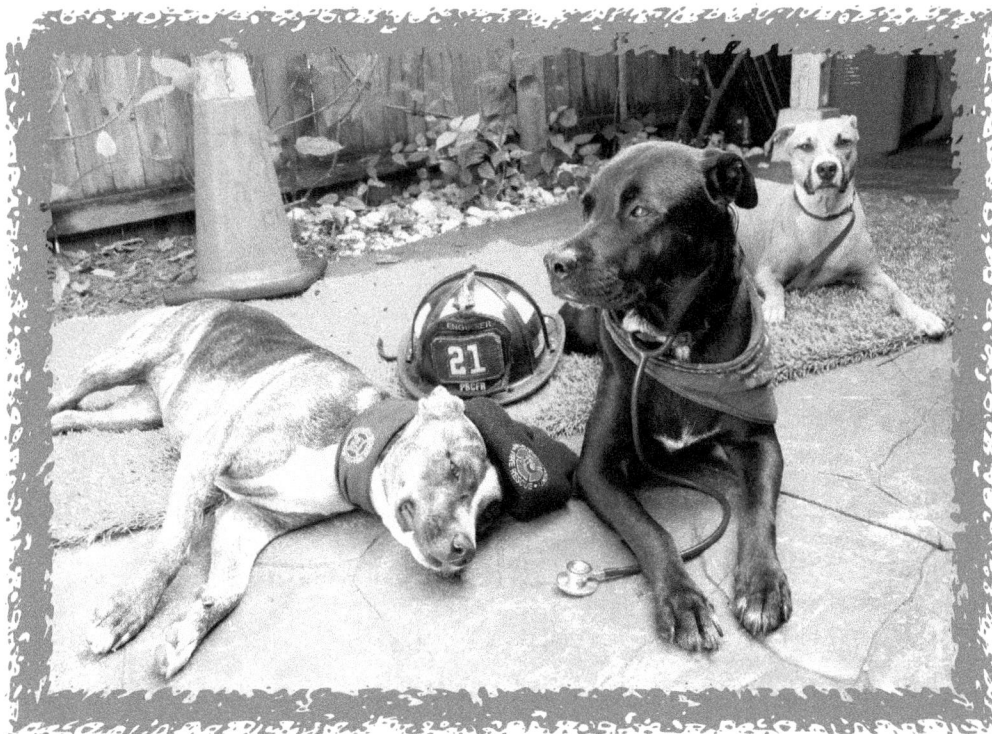

Acupressure

Many dog owners are not aware that dogs also respond to the application of pressure. In a dog that is having a seizure, the acupressure point is GV26, located right at the base of the nose where it meets the upper lip. Pressure for one minute at this point may put a halt to the seizure.

Comfort

Once the dog is out of the seizure, comfort him/her by talking in a soft reassuring tone and petting him/her. Massage some diluted lavender oil with water, because it is calming and healing. The added care will help the animal feel comforted instead of being disoriented upon awakening.

Getting Blood Sugar Levels Up

The use *Maple syrup, or orange juice* can help if a dog's sugar level drops below 60 mg. A dog having a low blood sugar level will cause your dog to exhibit symptoms of shakiness, unsteady walking, trembling lip. Hypoglycemia, or low blood sugar, is a potentially life-threatening situation for a dog. Insulin injections are given to diabetic pets to even out blood sugar levels.

Feeding Seizures

A seizure drains energy from dogs. Once the dog is acting normally, you can feed half the amount of regular food to your pet. Make sure your dog can effectively swallow safely. Avoid choking by slowing down ingestion. Monitor your dog carefully following a seizure.

Check Dogs Gums

Gums should be a nice bubble gum pink. If they are pale, consult with a vet.

If your dog appears to still not be doing well after half an hour, report it to your veterinarian. A veterinarian should be consulted if the animal has another seizure, or if the seizure lasts more than 5 minutes. If your dog is prone to seizures, they may need prescription Phenobarbital, Potassium Bromide or a combination of both. While they may help control the seizures, you should know that they can be extremely harmful to your dog's liver and other organs.

CBD

Like humans, dogs also have an endocannabinoid system, meaning they respond to cannabinoids in a similar way that we do. CBD is highly regarded as a well-tolerated supplement for many dogs. It can be used to treat epileptic seizures in dogs. Used as tinctured oil with a dropper. It is important to get full spectrum premium-grade like, CO_2 extracted, with no fillers, or sugar.

Chapter 2
Common Pets Emergencies

Antifreeze Poisoning

Drinking anti-freeze is a common cause of poisoning in dogs because of dogs like the way it tastes. It is easily accessible; found in driveways (from cars sitting overnight), garages and storage areas at your home. Anti-freeze can be fatally toxic to your pet. It can affect the brain, liver, and kidneys. Symptoms of antifreeze poisoning are drunken behavior, euphoria/delirium, wobbly, uncoordinated movement, nausea, vomiting, excessive urination, diarrhea, rapid heartbeat, depression, weakness, seizure, convulsions,

shaking tremors and fainting which could lead to coma. Contact your veterinarian immediately if your dog has any of these symptoms.

The treatment for immediate aid if you are positive that your dog has ingested antifreeze, is to try to induce vomiting by giving your dog hydrogen peroxide solution. Some toxic poisons will do more harm coming back through the esophagus. If your dog is unconscious do not try to induce vomiting. The amount of hydrogen peroxide recommended by various sources is one teaspoon per every 10 pounds of body weight.

Allergic Reaction and Sting Bites

These are most commonly seen in the summer months but can occur at any time of year. Typical signs are swelling around the eyes, face, or hives, most easily seen on the belly. These can be quite itchy for your pet. Severe allergic reactions can lead to breathing difficulty due to swelling of the airways. Other signs of a severe reaction include extensive swelling throughout the body, diarrhea, and shock. Severe reactions are more likely to be seen following multiple stings. If your pet is showing signs of discomfort or distress, contact your vet.

Bloat or Gastric Dilatation Volvulus (GDV)

GDV is where the stomach becomes twisted, it is probably the most serious non-trauma related emergency for any dog. The early signs may just be that a dog appears restless after a large meal and tries to vomit. As GDV develops your dog's abdomen will become distended or bloated and your dog will shows signs of discomfort, pain or hide and will continue to be sick. In most cases, all they will manage to bring up is white froth. They may drool excessively and you may notice an increase in breathing rate and heart rate. GDV is most commonly seen in large, deep chested breeds such as Great Danes or German Shepherds. If you suspect your dog has a GDV you must seek immediate veterinary treatment.

Boat Rides

In an open boat, with an open stretch from shore, you must practice water safety. You should have a doggy life jacket on your pet. Even though dogs can be excellent swimmers for short distances, they can drown from exhaustion if they swim a long distance, or for a long time. A life jacket will help keep a dog afloat if he/she should accidentally fall in. Keep in mind there are also rip currents that could be very dangerous. The US Coast Guard tells us we should have a life jacket on board for humans and that advice goes for animals traveling on the water too! It's very important to check that the life jacket has been tested and meets proper coast guard standards before you purchase it. Some dog life jackets can work against your dog being able to have their heads above the water.

Breathing Difficulties

If you notice wheezing, choking, weak and raspy breathing, shallow breathing or coughing. Breathing difficulties can result from foreign bodies in the throat, allergic reactions, asthma, heart disease or lung disease. Breathing problems are serious and potentially life-threatening, so get your pet seen as soon as possible.

Bufo Toad Poisoning

The first obvious sign your **dog** caught a **toad** is **foaming** at the **mouth**. He or she's mouth may get irritated and you will see your dog pawing at their mouth and shaking their head. If you see any frog that jumps and sticks to the wall, they are tree frogs. A **dog** and **toad** encounter can leave the **dog** with **mouth** pain, but a bufo toad can kill your dog within minutes.

The bufo toads emit a spray, and if your dog licks it, this could be fatal and should be treated with urgency. One symptom is a seizure.

Wash the dog's mouth out, with your dogs head below the body. This is so that the poison infected water washes out of your dogs mouth and not get swallowed. Do this as soon as possible. Follow by grabbing a towel and keep wiping clean until you get it all out and rush the animal to the closest emergency animal clinic.

Call your veterinarian and head down there with your pet. Here is the American Association of Poison Control Center open 24 hours everyday at 1-800-222-1222.

Car Accident Safety

A 60-pound unsecured dog traveling at 35 miles per hour can turn into a 2,700 pound projectile in a car accident. Keep your dog safe with the right travel harness and attach to a seat harness; one without tethers, so it allows your pet to sit and lay down.

Check out this video link on actual car accident tests for dogs that I found very interesting. I think you will too!

Dog Crash Test Video

According to American Humane, **_100,000 dogs are killed each year in accidents involving riding in truck beds_**. Veterinarians say they see numerous cases of

dogs injuring themselves jumping out, breaking legs and joint injuries that often result in amputation or hanging themselves, even being run over. Dogs can see something and want to go after it in traffic because they are reactive by nature. If you are in a car accident or have to brake suddenly your dog would be a shooting projectile.

It is also common for dogs jumping from inside the car, getting themselves killed and pets getting run over even on their property.

Car Trips

Avoid feeding your dog before you leave on a trip, as your pet may get nauseated and vomit. You should cover the floor or seats with towels or comforters or even newspapers. You should stop every 2 to 3 hours for a water or bathroom break and some exercise to relieve some of the stress. Roll windows up so that your dogs can't jump out and get killed. Also, make sure your dog can't open the car door and fall out. These are common occurrence.

Cystitis

If you notice your dog is straining to urinate frequently or if your dog is not producing any urine, they are having difficulty passing urine or you notice blood in the urine, you should immediately go see your veterinarian as soon as possible. It may be a sign that your pet has a life-threatening blockage (this is more common in males than females). More information on page 90.

Dog Bites

The safest, most effective way to stop a dog from biting and/or fighting, is a water hose. Use with caution. Dog bites can be lethal to an animal. If the bite causes a puncture to an animal, immediate first aid would be to apply pressure to the wound with clean towels, to stop any bleeding. Clean or wash gently with warm water and soap. You may have to repeat this several times. Dry the wound. Apply "dog-friendly" antibacterial topical ointment, then wrap with gauze and self-cling wrap. If there is any swelling, apply a cold pack or ice to the wound, and keep the dog calm. Having some self-adhesive first aid glue can be beneficial if done with in the first 12 hour period. Contact your veterinarian if the wound does not heal, close and drain fluid properly to avoid infections.

Dog Collapsing

This is described as a loss of strength that causes your pet to fall and/or be unable to rise. Common possible causes include; heart disease, vascular (vein and artery) disease, hemorrhage (internal or external bleeding), anemia, respiratory (lung) disease, neurological (brain or nerve) disease, musculoskeletal (muscle, ligament, tendon, bone) disease, toxicity in some drugs and medications. If your pet suffers any form of collapse seek immediate veterinary attention as there could be life-threatening.

Eye Problems

Eye (ocular) problems can deteriorate quickly and if left untreated can result in blindness or loss of the

eye. Signs of ocular disease include redness of the eye, discharge, excessive tearing, swelling, squinting or a closed eye and constant pawing at the eye. Even if it is just a foreign body in the eye or a superficial scratch to the cornea, prompt veterinary treatment can prevent a minor problem from becoming a serious one. You can reference one of my other Everything Dogs Books "Dogs Holistic Health and Natural Remedies Encyclopedia Book for some natural treatments.

Paraphimosis

Paraphimosis Education Video

Many times a dog can get excited playing with a toy, which can lead to an embarrassing situation for a dog owner. This can lead to your dog being unable to retract his penis (paraphimosis). This often occurs when the dog has a small opening (orifice), which in many cases is a birth defect that can be fixed. If the dog is unable to retract the penis (phimosis). It may have swelling or hairs that are obstructing the penis. This can, in some cases, lead to further injury.

This condition becomes more serious when irritation and dryness occur on the surface of the penis after the glans have protruded for an extensive amount of time before the pet is rush to the E R. Contact with environmental surfaces, like the ground or carpets can cause infection, which can lead to other complications, like bladder enlargement. This is very painful.

Resolving paraphimosis can be relatively simple, but can also be complex, depending on the length of time that the problem occurs and the amount of irritation, trauma or swelling occurring in the penis.

An owner can try **assisting with a cool sugar-water rinse** to reduce pressure from blood vessels, a cool wet washcloth or an application of **KY lubricant.** A sterile surgical grade highly-osmotic solution, like a 50% dextrose solution, can be applied to the surface to promote the movement of the penis. Gently try to press it back into the prepuce (or slide the prepuce forward over the glans).

If hair from the prepuce is sticking to the glans and preventing proper repositioning, carefully use an electric trimmer to trim away the hairs.

In a more severe scenario, the prepuce tissue may need to be surgically cut to create a larger opening for the penis to be retracted. Obviously, this is for a veterinary professional to perform the treatment if retraction is beyond the owner's ability to lubricate and readily replace the penis to its natural position.

Poisoning by Indiscrete Ingestion

If you are concerned your dog has eaten something inappropriate, call your vet immediately for advice. The most common poisonings we see are *chocolate, grapes, raisins, human medications, lilies, rat and slug poisons.* Some of these poisonings *can be successfully treated* if immediately caught. These can turn into life-threatening situations once your pet starts to absorb the poisons in their digestive system.

Rat Poison

This is the number one most popular poison because it is made to taste good. Pet owners always claim their dog couldn't have had come in contact with it. Pets will find a way to get to it because it also smells good to them. If you see them eat it, give them a teaspoon or two of hydrogen peroxide. If they throw up green that means they are getting it out of their body. Your vet should be contacted immediately. Symptoms, like bleeding, may not appear for a couple of weeks. Vitamin K is used for treatment.

Rawhide

This picture is of my registered pedigree German Shepherd Hawkeye. He died in my Jeep as a result of obstruction from a rawhide product twisting in his stomach. This is very common. There was nothing I could do to get him to a veterinarian on time to save him.

Rawhide bones can be an inadvertent source of death for your pet.

- Tiny pieces of rawhide, when swallowed, can cause swelling in your pet's digestive system. This can lead to internal intestinal blockage. It can be fatal to your pet. Rawhide is indigestible and can cause serious illness.

- Poisonous chemicals are used in the manufacturing of rawhide products.

- The extremely tough texture is known to be a serious choking hazard.

- Symptoms are vomiting, diarrhea and a swollen stomach.

Risk of Rabies

Rabies is a virus commonly carried in raccoons, bats and foxes. This virus is transmitted through saliva in bites from rabid animals. A symptom of a rabid infection is excessive salivation and should be considered a warning sign. Humans can also be at risk of infection from rabid dog bites. This is why it is mandated for dogs to have rabies vaccination.

If you are traveling out of the country with your dog, you will be required to have your dog's rabies vaccination up to date. Some countries require rabies quarantine for many months. It's highly recommended that you keep a copy of your pet's rabies vaccination with you.

Retractable Leash

The length of some retractable leashes can extend up to 26 feet. In my opinion, it allows a dog to get too far ahead from the owner, putting them in a situation that can quickly turn dangerous. A dog could easily run into the middle of the street or initiate contact with other dogs. They can engage in fighting when given too much slack on the leash. Long leads can also snap, tangle and cause neck injury, get pulled out of your hand or cause bystanders to trip and fall. Retractable leashes teach a dog to pull far from the safe zone of their owner. Leashes over 10 feet should be used specifically for training your dog the "Come Command".

Urinating Problem or Cystitis

If you notice your dog is not producing any urine, trying to urinate frequently, is experiencing difficulty passing urine, you notice blood in the urine, it may be a sign that your pet has cystitis or a life-threatening blockage. This is known to be more common in males than in females. Straining to urinate is a symptom of many urinary tract infections. One possible cause might be from crystals or stones in their bladder. Inflammation, blood clots, cancer or even stress alone can also cause difficulty with urination. If a pet is straining and is unable to pass any urine, it is a life-threatening emergency, that needs to be addressed by a veterinarian immediately.

Vomiting or Diarrhea

Vomiting and diarrhea are common problems in dogs. While they can be signs of a serious illness the majority of cases are simple stomach upsets. It typically resolves within 24 hours. If your dog develops any other signs such as lethargy or weakness, seems to be in pain, vomiting or diarrhea persists for more than 24 hours and you notice blood in the vomit or the diarrhea then go to see your vet immediately.

Diarrhea may also be accompanied by vomiting, loss of appetite, weight loss, abdominal pain, lethargy, and other symptoms of disease which is often due to scavenging behavior, stress, a sudden change in diet, viral, bacterial or parasitic infections.

More chronic diarrhea can be caused by dietary allergies or intolerances, stress, some types of parasites (Giardia, hookworms, roundworms and whipworms), bacterial infections, pancreatic disease, inflammatory bowel disease, irritable bowel syndrome, some types of cancer and diseases outside of the gastrointestinal tract leading to liver failure or heart disease.

Milk and Dairy Products

Known as common triggers for food allergies in dog's milk or all dairy can appear as irritation of the **skin, redness, itching and GI upset, such as vomiting, and diarrhea**.

While most dogs will readily drink milk, we should consider the consequence that milk does to our furry family member. When dogs are puppies, they drink their mother's milk. That is the only time they should drink milk. This is because milk contains a sugar called lactose that requires an enzyme called lactase for digestion. Puppies generally have this enzyme in abundance. This is used to breakdown their mother's milk while nursing. While puppies thrive on their mother's milk, they may not tolerate cow or goat milk.

Recommendations:

•Remove all food for 12 hours

•Make sure the dog has access to plenty of clean water to avoid dehydration. Encourage the dog to drink. If needed, offer diluted broth or coconut water in addition to the water.

•Give the dog a small meal of white rice and broth. This can be the dog's diet until the stool consistency returns to normal.

••If diarrhea continues for more than 24 hours, or your dog's condition worsens at any time, call your vet immediately.

How to Avoid a Recurrence of Dog Diarrhea

- Do not suddenly change a dog's diet.

- Do not give the dog bones as toys.

- Do not feed your dog table scraps like animal fats and cooked bones that can splinter or cause a obstruction.

- Do not allow your dog to scavenge.

- Always keep your dog up-to-date with deworming and vaccinations.

Chapter 3
Dogs
Over Heating

A dog's natural temperature is between 101 - 102.5°F. Dogs do not lose body heat by sweating. They have a small quantity of sweat glands, that are located in the paw pads. Their primary source of heat exchange is by panting. Because of this, they can suffer from heatstroke and die quickly. This is an agonizing death that can happen within minutes and is avoidable.

The most common cause of overheating is when people leave their fur dog children in their car with the windows up on a hot summer day. The heat rises quickly in a closed-up vehicle and it is lethal. Contact the local authorities to get help immediately.

Environmental factors can also place a dog at risk. Be aware not just of high temperatures, but also of high humidity. This can increase the chance of heat exhaustion in dogs causing them to become over-heated, excessively salivate and pant. A dog may experience convulsions, exhibit vomiting, diarrhea, and may also have gums, or a tongue, that turns blue, or bright red. Your dog may not respond to commands and collapse.

Just walking your dog in the middle of the day can cause your dog to overheat. Older dogs are especially sensitive to this.

Things to do:

- **Remove the dog from the hot location.** Immediately place them in a cool shaded or air-conditioned area. You can put your dog in the bathtub and run cool water, especially on the head neck, and armpits area.

- *Clear the mouth of saliva to help to breath.* Then use a sponge or wet towel that has been saturated with cool (but not ice cold) water and wrap the dog's body in it.

- *Cool downs can be facilitated using a garden hose* or placement in a pool of cool water. Cold packs and even a packet of frozen vegetables work fine to relieve heat from the body.

- *Get their circulation going by massaging the legs* vigorously. Rubbing helps to reduce the risk of shock.

- *Continue pouring cool water over the body* to reduce heating. Focus on the head and neck area, and under the armpits.

- *Hydrate by providing water* for the dog to get hydrated and drink. Squeeze the water from a wet towel into his mouth.

- Check for dehydration in your dog's gums, by pulling up his lip/cheek. Then push down on his gums above his teeth to see how quickly the color comes back. It should come back immediately.

•Take your dog's temperature every five minutes, continuing water-cooling until it drops below 103°F (39.4°C). If your dog's temperature drops a little more, to around 100°F (37.8°C), don't worry. A slightly low temperature is a lot less dangerous.

•Get immediate veterinary attention. Heatstroke can cause unseen problems, such as swelling of the brain, kidney failure and abnormal clotting of blood may occur.

On the way to the veterinarian, travel with the windows open and the air conditioner on. The veterinarian hospital or doctor can get the pet hydrated with IV fluids to stabilize their condition. Unfortunately, some dogs won't recover. This can be serious and life-threatening for an animal. Immediate and proper actions are recommended.

Always keep your dogs hydrated!

Chapter 4
Water Toxification on Dogs

My Foster Puppies! Reunion Party Video!

Make sure that your dog does not have any open wounds before going swimming. For instance, in Florida there have been numbers of potentially deadly bacteria outbreaks reported in our coastal waters. It's also been reported that people and dogs die from going in the water while visiting. If your pet has open wounds, you are cautioned to stay out of the water. Water toxicity can also be a possibility in a poorly maintained chlorinated pool.

It's important to keep in mind that serious illness resulting from swimming is very rare in dogs. The most important health risk to pups in the pool or pond is drowning. However, if your pet shows signs of illness after a swim, please take him or her in for a check-up.

Diseases from Water

Blue/Green Algae

Any contact with Blue/Green Algae can cause severe effects on pets and people. Symptoms include; skin, GI tract, liver, and central nervous system can also be affected. Contact with a bloom should be immediately reported to your veterinarian, as death can occur in severe cases.

Cryptosporidiosis

This is a condition caused by species of Cryptosporidium, which exist in different animal species and some can cross-infect humans. The parasite is protected in the environment by a thick outer shell, which makes it able to survive in an environment for a long time. It is resistant to chlorine and disinfectants. It is one of the most common water-borne diseases linked to recreational water. Dogs are infected by ingesting the infected oocysts in contaminated food or water. Crypto causes watery diarrhea, which can lead to severe dehydration. Fortunately, for dogs, most cases are mild or subclinical and are rarely life-threatening. Symptoms usually resolve within two weeks with appropriate treatment.

Giardiasis

Exposure can cause severe dehydration and weight loss if infected for long periods. Most cases of Giardia are mild and self-limiting. Symptomatic treatment and medications can speed up recovery in affected pets.

Leptospirosis

Leptospirosis is known world-wide to affect both humans and animals. There are many strains. The disease can be life-threatening if untreated. Many dogs respond well to early treatment with supportive care and antibiotics.

Schistosomiasis, Heterobilharzia Americana

Commonly known as the flatworm is the causativeagent of canine schistosomiasis. The organism penetrates the skin of the dog while swimming or wading in contaminated freshwater. It then migrates through the lungs into the liver. While this organism does not live in humans, the parasites can burrow into the skin and cause a rash known as "swimmer's itch."

Rodger in Pool with Floaters Adoption Video!

Pseudomonas Aeruginosa

This is the most common organism associated with chronic ear infections in dogs. It causes a smelly, oozy, odor and a substantial amount of painful swelling. Pseudomonas are frequently found in pools and is thought to be a common cause of "swimmer's ear". Owners whose dogs are prone to ear infections can usually see this coming by the shaking head, the scratching at the ear canals, the stinky head. It is one of the most common reasons dogs are brought to the veterinary clinic. While *otitis externa i*s a disease with multiple causes, such as bacteria, yeast, and underlying allergies. Be aware of those causative agents that can be found in water.

Pythiosis

A tropical spore with the nickname "swamp cancer", which says it all. Pythiosis of the lungs, brain or sinus will show signs in the dog as; stuffiness, head pain, fever, coughing and swelling of the sinuses. An infection of the dog's digestive tract can lead to chronic disease.

Here are some adoption videos of our time together:

Reporting Post Hurrican Mathew Adoption Video!

Coco & Mindy's Halloween Adoption Video!

Obstacle Course - Coco's Adoption Video!

What to do if your Pet is Choking

Toys or other home objects that are too small for your dog to play with are hazardous because they can get stuck in your dog's throat. Food can also become caught in the back of the throat, thus blocking their air supply.

Symptoms are distress, deep labored breathing, (you could hear that something sounds stuck in their throat), from something blocking the airway as your dog tries to take a breath. If the dog is suffocating, they will often panic. Dogs may paw at their mouth as if something is lodged. Choking is a possibility in an unresponsive or unconscious dog. In these cases, throat and mouth should be checked for foreign objects. *If your dog is unconscious, check for air movement and heartbeat. I recommend practicing how and where to find the pulse of an animal before an emergency occurs.*

*Perform CPR if your pet is not choking and not breathing.

If you feel you can dislodge the item yourself, proceed with caution. Inspect the mouth. A break stick may be needed to keep the mouth open while trying to remove the stuck object. Needle-nosed pliers or forceps could be used to help remove the lodged object as well.

How to Help a Choking Dog

Look, feel & listen.

There are a few thing you can do before performing the famous Heimlich that are in the following diagram, in steps 1 through 8, to dislodge the blockage and open air-ways. You must act quickly!

Let's get started!

Step 1
RECOGNIZE YOUR PET IS CHOKING BY IDENTIFYING THE SITUATION

Call for anyone around that may be able to *help.*

Step 2
INSPECT BY MOUTH OPENING

Look in the mouth, sweep the back of the throat. If you can see something lodged in the throat, *sweep side to side to see if you can grab it to dislodge the object.* The use of needle-nosed pliers or forceps can help to get the object out if you can see it or grab it!

Step 3
FINGER SWEEP

By Hooking your finger around the back of the object. Use caution with your hands.

Step 4
WHEEL CART

By Clasping your hands around the upper stomach, under the rib cage. You can also lift the dog upside down, so that gravity could help with pressure to get the object out. Grab ahold of the dog by locking your hands together between bottom ribs in the top part of the stomach, with your stomach on the animal's back and *pull five times.*

Step 5
REPEAT STEPS
1 AND 2 - Open mouth to inspect inside and finger sweeping from side to side until you can dislodge the object.

Step 6
A SHARP BLOW

Carefully give a sharp thrust inward and upward, between the shoulders, to help dislodge the object.

If the dog is too large and is laying down, *come around behind and put your arms around them, clasping your hands together pushing inward and upward between the bottom rib and the top of the stomach.* Repetition may be necessary.

7. REPEAT 1 AND 2 - By opening mouth and finger sweeping. If necessary, proceed with the Heimlich maneuver.

Heimlich

Clasp your hands together and squeeze your pet's abdomen inward and upward, by the rib cage, to force the object out. Like *Step 4, Wheel Cart. on pictures*

If you still can't get the object out, flip your dog upside down and repeat if necessary to dislodge object till your pet can breathe again, like on the following page.

Remember to always reward your dog after such a trauma. Love and affection is a great reward for your dog.

Chapter 6
CPR
Cardiopulmonary Resuscitation

It is very important to first determine if the dog is breathing. A dog may have collapsed and can be unconscious, but may still be breathing. So make sure that CPR is necessary before taking action.

Check out Everything Dogs "How to do CPR on Your Dog" here.

How to do CPR Demo Video!

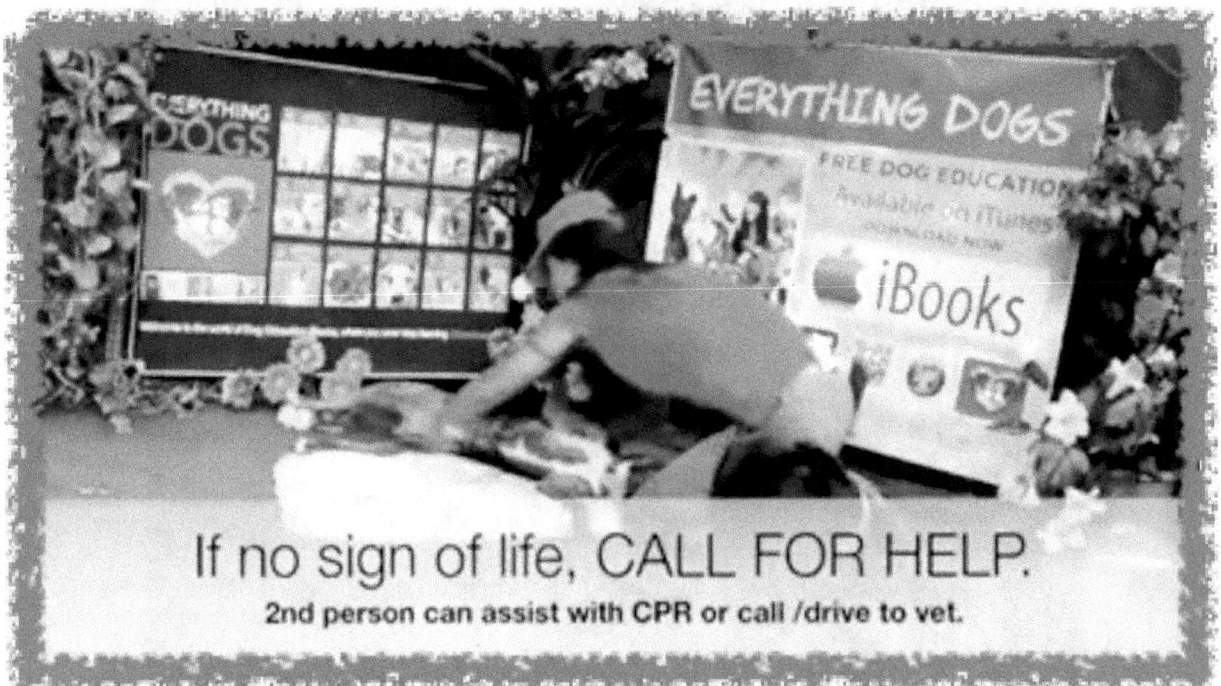

If no sign of life, CALL FOR HELP.
2nd person can assist with CPR or call /drive to vet.

In an emergency, you will want to remember your A, B, C's of CPR!

This is when knowing the ABC's of Doggie CPR can save a life & have best chance of survival.

A is for **Airway**

B is for **Breathing.**

C is for **Circulation and Chest Compressions.**

1- CHECK TO SEE IF ANIMAL IS BREATHING AND HAS A HEARTBEAT

Open Air way, pull tongue out, look in, do a finger sweep

to pull the object out you may need tweezers or forceps.

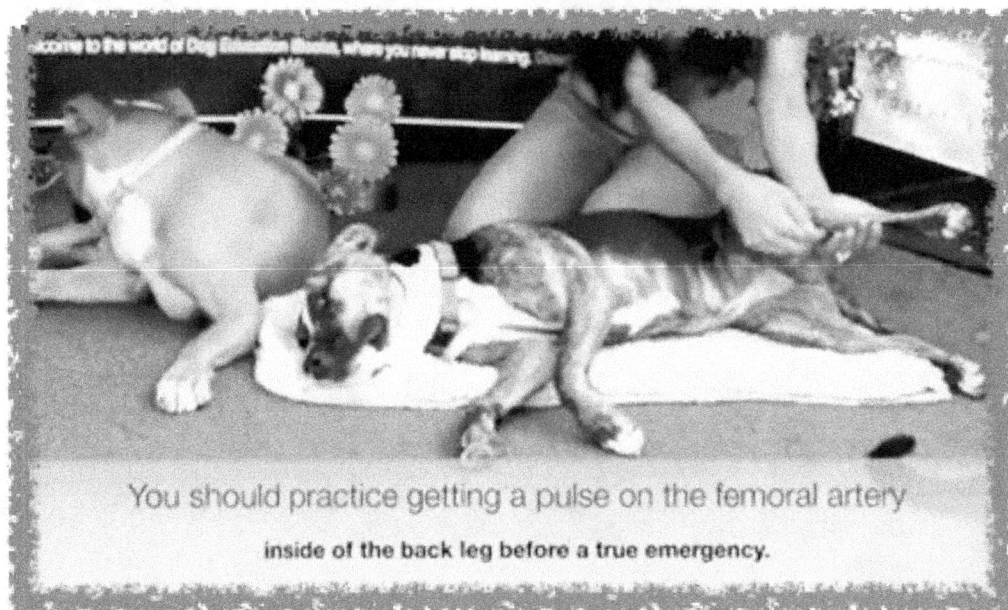

You should practice getting a pulse on the femoral artery

inside of the back leg before a true emergency.

You should practice how to find your pet's pulse before a true emergency.

2- YOU MUST MAKE SURE YOU HAVE AN OPEN AIRWAY BEFORE STARTING CPR

There may be something blocking the dog's throat and causing an obstruction. This will interfere with the resuscitation process. The blockage could be caused by vomit, blood, mucus, or foreign material.

3- LOOK FOR WARNING SIGNS LIKE:

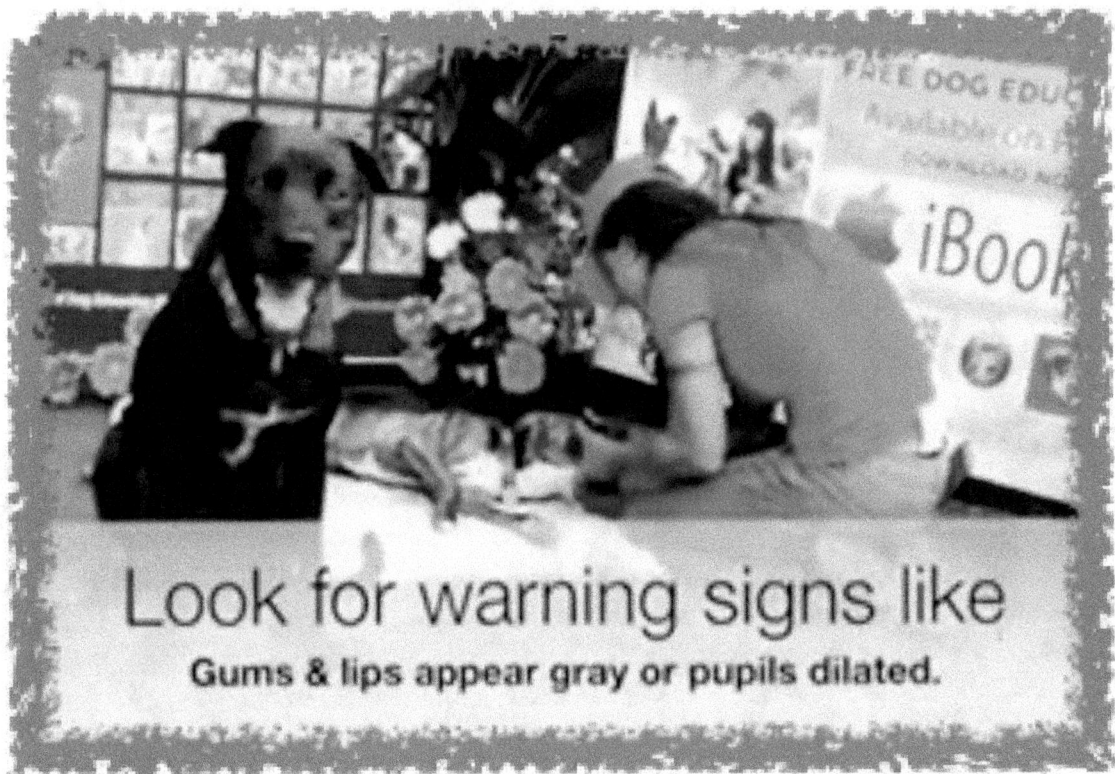

Look for warning signs like
Gums & lips appear gray or pupils dilated.

Gums and lips will appear gray or pupils will be dilated.

4- START CHEST COMPRESSIONS ONLY IF THERE IS "NO PULSE" AND NOTHING BLOCKING AIR PATH.

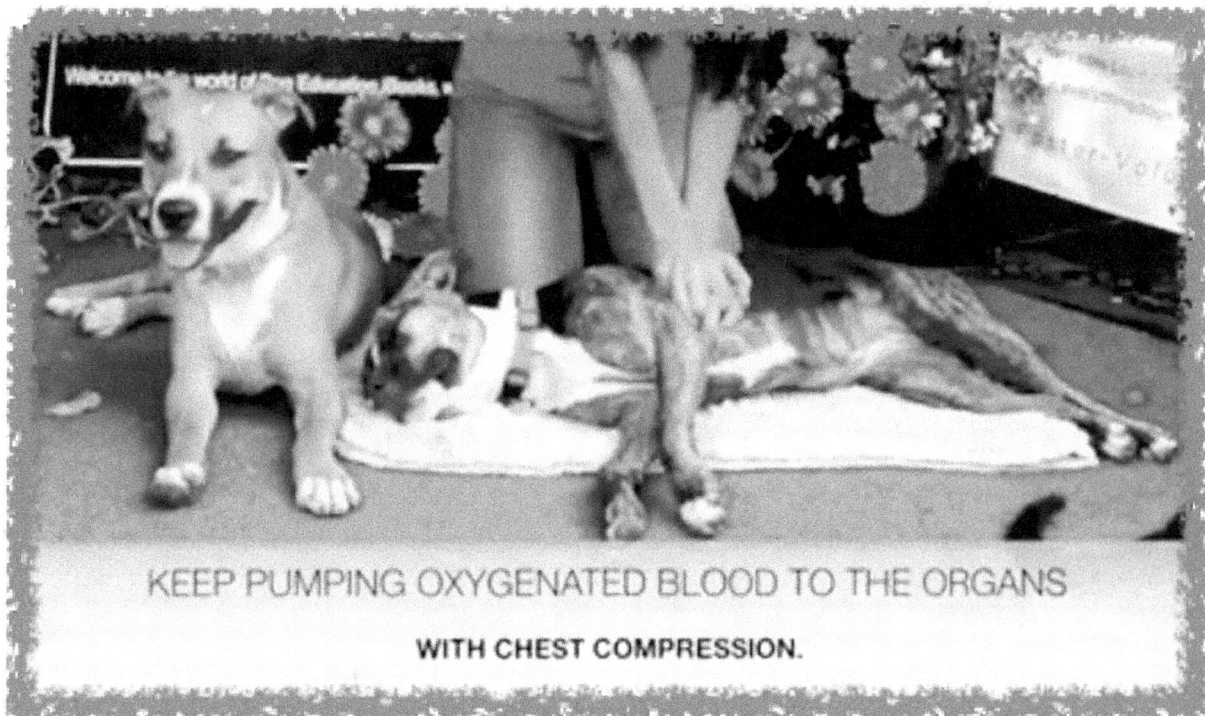

KEEP PUMPING OXYGENATED BLOOD TO THE ORGANS WITH CHEST COMPRESSION.

Begin by laying animal on their right side and swing its elbow back to the point where it meets the chest wall. That point is the 3rd to 5th intercostal space where the heart lies. Place one hand over the other, on the rib area, where its elbow touches the chest. Begin compression immediately.

DO NOT PERFORM CPR IF YOUR DOG HAS A PULSE.

With 2 people -15 compressions followed by 2 full breaths.

You may switch positions, but keep rhythm going uninterrupted.

DOGS, 30-90 lbs., 5 chest compressions per breath. **LARGE DOG**, over 90 lbs., 10 compressions per breath.

PUPPIES AND SMALLER ANIMALS: Place your thumb and forefingers of both hands around the puppy's chest just behind the front legs where the heart is located.

5- IF NOT BREATHING START MOUTH -TO- MOUTH

- Cats, small dogs, and medium-large dogs: Place your mouth over nose and mouth, then blow air.

- **Large dogs:** You will blow in air through the nose only. Make sure that the mouth is shut so that air does not escape. Do 20 to 30 breaths a minute or one every two or three seconds.

6- WATCH CHEST WALLS LIFT - Stop blowing once the chest has lifted. If you continue blowing you may damage the dog's lungs.

- Check the dog to see if the lungs are getting filled with air by putting your hand on the dog's chest to feel the rise of breath.

- If the chest does not lift, it is because something is blocking the airway.

7- KEEP PUMPING OXYGENATED BLOOD TO THE ORGANS WITH CHEST COMPRESSIONS. You are now giving artificial

respiration, but there may be no heartbeat. The oxygen can't get to where it's needed and you'll need to provide chest compression for artificial recirculation.

Stop blowing once chest has lifted.

REPEAT PROCEDURE - Check pulse after 1 minute and every few minutes. Continue giving CPR until an animal has a pulse or is breathing.

Stop after 20 minutes.

Chapter 7
Dog Fire Hazard

It is estimated that there are more than 500,000 house fires a year.

The National Fire Protection Association estimates that nearly 1,000 house fires each year are accidentally started by the homeowner's pets. This is because dogs get very interested in the food left on kitchen stoves and in an attempt to snag a taste, they accidentally ignite items left on stovetops to get food or just because they are curious.

This is Hank. He had severe damage from burns on his back. He was adopted!

Precaution to take From Your Pet Starting a Dangerous Fire

Stove Knobs

Even if your pet is not prone to jumping on counters, you can remove your stove knobs or use covers to protect them. Keep everything off the stove, when you leave your pets at home alone, you can also restrict their access to the kitchen. *The most common pet fire is started by starting a stove.*

Collars and Leashes

Make sure you always leave leashes and collars in plain sight and readily available at entrances in case your pet needs to be rescued.

Electrical Cords

Pets, who chew on electrical cords, can suffer from severe injuries, and can also start to be a fire hazard. This is common with puppies and bored anxious dogs.

Open Flames

Never leave your pet alone near an open flame. Whether you're grilling in the backyard or enjoying your fireplace. Make sure you completely extinguish all open fires before leaving your house.

Extinguish Open Flames

Pets are generally curious and will investigate cooking appliances, candles or even a fire in your fireplace. Ensure your pet is not left unattended around an open flame and make sure to thoroughly extinguish any open flame before leaving your home.

Flameless Candles

Investing in these candles that contain a light bulb instead of an open flame. These can take the danger out of your pet knocking over a lit candle.

Secure Young Pets

Keep them confined away from potential fire-starting hazards when you are away from home, such as in crates or behind baby gates in secure areas.

Help Firefighters
Find Your Pets

• Keep pets near entrances when away from home.

• Keep collars and leashes at access to firefighters in case your pets need rescue.

• Place Pet Alert Identification Sticker (you can find in many fire stations) or a Window Cling type of sign on your front door or front window listing the number of dogs and or cats that live in your home and names. This will help alert firefighter to search and rescue for your furry family member at a time of a fire emergency. The critical information saves rescuers time when locating your pets is crucial. Make sure to keep the number of pets listed up-dated always. You can place one of these inside your door too. If you do not have these stickers, it can result in a injury to your pet because rescuers won't know to look for your animals.

Emergency
Pet Plan

Pets who suffer injuries from a fire should be rushed to an emergency pet hospital.

• The best way to protect your pets from the effects of a fire is to include them in your family plan. This includes having their own disaster first aid kit as well as arranging in advance for a safe place for them to stay if you need to leave your home.

• When you practice your escape plan, practice taking your pets with you.

• Train them to come to you when you call their name.

• In the event of a disaster, if you must evacuate, the most important thing you can do to protect your pets is to evacuate them with you.

Chapter 8
Strangulation by Dog Collar

"Flower" at the Shelter, learning to trust again.

Dog collar accidents are very common resulting in death. Wearing dog collars can be hazardous in a the situation. Dog collars and tags can become entangled or caught between many things like the wires of his or her crate, kitchen cabinets, fencing, furniture. Even while playing with another dog can be very dangerous for both dogs and you too. Dogs can jump up and snag their collar on a fence post or a window latch or blinds, leading to suffocation.

Even a well-fitting collar can be dangerous if used to tie up a dog in the backyard. It's common for dogs who are tied up to jump fences while tied on a long leash and end up hanging themselves with their collar.

When a dog panics, this can cause a dog to choke himself. You will likely need very sharp scissors or a knife to cut the collar off.

Strangulation by collar is very common and has caused many dogs to lose their lives.

On the right me with a neighbors dog

Because of Dog Collars Accidents are so Common

Large pet retail companies created break-away snap collars because dogs choking with their collar are so common. Break-Away Collars are highly recommended. Make sure it is a reliable one because some brands can easily become open when you need to have control over your dog the most. When this happens, you have a loose dog situation, because you trusted the collar to stay on your dog.

Strict collar removal from dogs policies is set in place in many pet-related businesses to remove collars from dogs like:

• For a veterinary technician it is mandatory to remove all collars from any patient in a kennel.

• Large retail grooming chains have strict policies requiring dog collars to be removed before dogs are placed in their kennels. Their collars are then placed in a plastic sleeve outside of the dog's crate.

Dogs should only wear a collar under supervision. That means you should take your dog's collar off whenever they're crated, playing with other dogs or left unsupervised in your home.

Collars Fitting

Loose Collars

Known to cause limb or mouth injuries. If a pet scratches their ear, their back leg or their front leg could get stuck inside the collar, looped through, leading to a limb breaking. Dogs can also get their teeth or tongue stuck in a collar as well while grooming themselves. This could lead to broken teeth and other mouth injuries.

Tight Collar

A collar that is too tight can be harmful to a dog and can lead to skin irritation, hair loss. The skin in those areas can be more prone to infection.

- In extreme cases, a very tight collar, it can cut into a dog's neck. This can happen in cases of neglect when a puppy collar is left on a growing dog or abandoned for long periods neglected.

- In general, to protect your pup's neck, regularly check that the collar still fits well. It's recommend to let your dog sleep at night without a collar so that your d**og's skin can air out.**

Neck Damage

Collars can harm a dog's neck if you pull too hard on the leash or if you use the collar to pull your dog around. The neck and throat are extremely sensitive areas. Repeated stress on the neck can even lead to long-term medical issues, including damaging the thyroid glands, tissues around the neck area and salivary glands.

A chest harness or Gentle Leader can be a safer alternative to neck collars that put a lot of strain on a dog's neck.

General Discomfort

Even if a collar does not lead to any serious injuries, the wrong collar can simply be irritating for a dog.

Pet owners should avoid a collar that looks rigid and uncomfortable because your dog should have a positive experience when your dogs have it on and enjoy the feeling.

Collar Safety Tips

When sizing a collar, make sure you can fit your thumb between the collar and the dog's neck. If the dog sits down or rolls over, their skin and body fat are redistributed, possibly resulting in the collar being too tight.

Constricting Collars

Keep it loose enough to slip two fingers under the collar. If your dog pulls excessively on the leash and chokes or coughs, your dog could *benefit from being trained to stop pulling* through the use of a head halter or harness that is specially designed to reduce pulling. Training is highly recommended.

Benefits of
Microchip vs Collars

The main reason dogs wear a collar is to carry ID tags with their pet owners contact information and current rabies mandated vaccination tag in case your dog becomes lost. Your dog can also be stolen from your home and/or property or even mistaken for an unwanted dog, where someone just keeps your

dog. Having a microchip can offer some protection as if they become lost, the finder can bring the dog to a veterinarian clinic or shelter to have the dog scanned. This is why it's even a better reason to get your dog microchipped.

If your pet gets out often, you should consider buying a **dog tracker** online for your pet, as well as making sure all your homes windows, doors, and property fences are 100% secure from your dog getting out by digging under or is too low for your dog to easily jump over. Some dogs like to climb over and sliding in between gates to get out. Dogs may even know how to open gates. In any case, collars can be taken off, fall off or ID tags can be lost. The microchips are underneath your dog's skin. It can't be removed. I recommend occasionally check your dog's microchip to make sure that your information is correct and that it can be read. I had two of my dog's microchips scan tested out a while ago, and no information was reading. I wouldn't have known if i had not asked to check it out! So please, go the extra mile for your dog by verifying that it is properly working and that the contact information is currently correct.

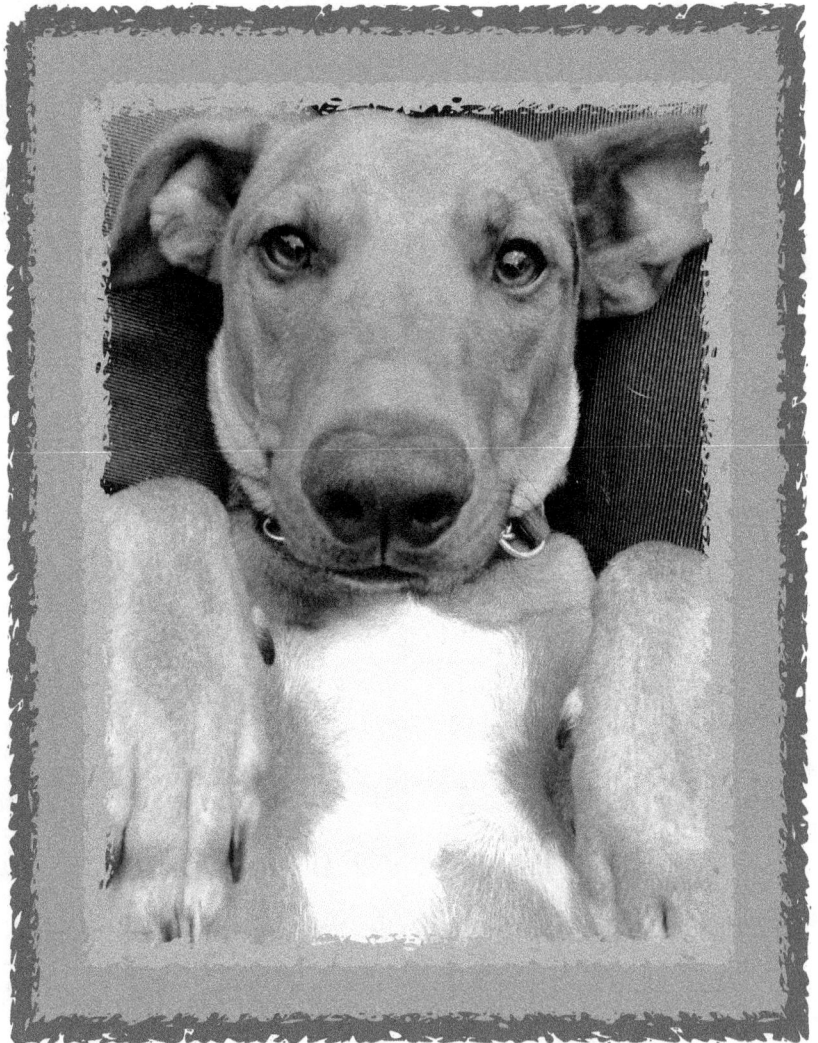

Chapter 9
Dog Attack Facts and Children

Dogbite.org studies 1982 and 2014 is the most detailed and current data.

- 4.5 - 4.7million people have been bitten by dogs in the United States. That is 2% of the US population. One out of every five gets infected.

- 50% of kids will be bitten by age 12. Almost one in five people bitten by dogs require medical attention.

- Every year, more than 800,000 Americans receive medical attention for dog bites; at least half of them are children.

- Annual data from 2014 shows that 48% (20) of the fatality victims were children 13 years and younger, and 52% (22) were adults, 20-years and older. Of the total adults killed by dogs in 2014, 73% (16) were ages 50-years and older.

- In 2014, 19% (8), of all dog bite fatality victims were either visiting or living temporarily with the dog's owner when the fatal attack occurred, down from 38% in 2013. Children 6-years and younger accounted for 88% (7) of these deaths.

- 57% (24) of all fatalities in 2014 involved more than one dog; 19% (8) involved a pack attack of four or more dogs; 31% (13) involved breeding on the dog owner's property either actively or in the recent past and 5% (2) involved tethered dogs.

- 76% of attacks result in fatalities.

- Dog ownership information for 2014 shows that family dogs comprised 48% (20) of all fatal attack occurrences, 40% (17) of the attacks occurred off the dog owner's property, up from 22% in 2013, and 21% (9) resulted in criminal charges.

- In the 1980s and 1990s, the US averaged 17 fatalities per year, while in the 2000s, this has increased to 26.

- 77% of dog bites are from the pet of family or friends and 50% of attacks occur on the dog owner's property.

- Dog ownership information for 2014 shows that family dogs comprised 48% (20) of all fatal attack occurrences, 40% (17) of the attacks occurred off the dog owner's property, up from 22% in 2013, and 21% (9) resulted in criminal charges.

- Animal bites, most of which are from dogs, are the reason for 1% of visits to an emergency department in the United States.

- 86% that result in maiming - it's very common for dog owners to get bit while breaking up their dogs from fighting.

- 6% of the attacks result in fatalities.

- Most dog bites affecting young children occur during everyday activities and while interacting with familiar dogs. Never leave your child alone because even though your dog is a good dog he or she can be easily be provoked. Senior citizens are the second most common dog bite victims.

- In the 1980s and 1990s, the US averaged 17 fatalities per year. While in the 2000s, this has increased to 77% of dog bites are from the pet of family or friends. 50% of attacks occur on the dog owner's property

- You must be calm and talk normally to the dog. Meaning no high pitched baby talk, because it could frighten the dog more.

- Close your hand, offer it for the dog to smell and then calmly pet the dog. He or she will let you know if they want you to pet them and proceed to pet by going under the neck area. Never go to pet over their heads; they may feel over powered, scared because they are not familiar with you, or just be a very skittish dogs.

- Never scare a dog sleeping, make a noise first or say their name. Don't approach a dog that is eating. He will defend what he believes is his property.

- Don't run from a dog. The chase instinct is very strong in dogs. Walk away slowly. If you can, walk backwards and don't turn your back until the dog has lost interest in you.

- Don't try to pet a dog by sticking your hand through a fence or into a crate. The dog may see this as an intrusion into his territory.

- Every dog has the potential to bite a human. Any canine that is threatened, hurt or scared can become a dangerous dog.

- Properly training, socializing your pet and educating your children on how to approach interacting with a dog will avoid dog bites; ranging from investing your time with your dog and in basic training. Making sure your dog walks well by not pulling when you walk your dog outside your property can avoid future potential dangerous situations. Having a plan is very important.

Chapter 10
Walking Safely
Prevention, Defense & Protection

Do not walk a dog that is too big for you to restrain. You do not have control of a dog if the dog can pull you off your feet, or drags you where your pet wants to go. The same caution applies for letting your child hold the leash, or walk the dog alone. Do not use a retractable leash, unless it's safe for your dog to lunge the full length of the leash, (away from you) and always have one hand occupied in holding the box part. Many dogs has been run over because a retractable leash allowed them to dash into the street. Many dogs have run off in panic when the owner dropped the box, then fleeing ever further to escape this plastic object that is was following them (the retractable leash box).   Also, if the re-tractable leash gets tangled while meeting another dog, this could result in a fight, that otherwise would not have tak-en place.

• It's better not to do "dog to

dog" greetings when walking your dog unless you know both the dogs are good at greeting on a leash because they know they can not flee, if they need too. Leashed dogs can be defensive when meeting new dogs on a leash. The same goes for letting children greet or pet your leashed dog.

- When walking your dog, it is most important to be familiar with the territory that you are planning to walk. Some people may have loose dogs on their property; their dogs may be very protective guard dogs and it may be too late, before you could

avoid a possible dog attack. If you are walking past bushes, you could be walking right into a loose dog: ready to attack! They may have heard you coming from down the street and are already in a position to attack.

- Chances are that an attacking dog will first be coming at your dog, and then you. If you have more than one dog, this could heighten the attack and be more dangerous; where your dogs could all get loose and cause an accident. It is important to know what is around you so that you can avoid a confrontation with any loose dogs.

- Always assume, if you can't see what is ahead of you, that there could be a situation, just a few feet from you that you may be walking into. Corners can be very dangerous; if you can't see what is around the corner, you don't know what you could be running into. Always keep your space and distance, so that you are not putting you and your dog at risk. Remember this can leave you with very little time to respond and in a dangerous situation.

- **Avoid walking past fenced yards with dogs** because the dogs on the property could jump, climb the fence, or even dig a fast hole to get at you. If you see a dog trying to jump a fence, hopefully, it is from the other side of the street and firmly and calmly tell the dog, "No!" Every dog should know the **"No"** word. Repeat and repeat again!

- **Avoid walking on county roads,** train tracks, vacant lots, field or anywhere dogs may roam free.

- **Never trust other people walking their dog,** especially if the leash looks tight from the dog pulling them. This will only make the dog want to lunge toward you more. Dog owners think that their dog would never bite, but that is not always true.

- **Give special attention to coming around a corner:** Again, always be prepared for anything. You might find yourself heading right into a loose dog that heard you coming and you may have little time to react defensively. Do not walk your dog too far ahead of you. Keep them on a 4-6 ft. leash at most because you would be putting your dog in a situation you can't avoid. By coming too close and too fast into an unknown attacking dog is very startling. This is a good reason to not wear head seats with loud music playing.

- **When night walking, you need to always be visible**. Have your dog wear a reflective dog collar, leash tags and clothing, so that cars and people can see you and your dog. Have a **flashlight** handy, so that you can see where you are walking. LED blinking flashlights work best.

- I recommend carrying an **"electric whistle"** or a "taser". Test it before every walk and make sure you have a fully charged battery and it that works. When a dog hears the taser's noise (based on my experience), the attacking dog will usually back off and head in the other direction. Always have your taser easily accessible. If using a pepper or citronella spray, you will need to aim for their nose. Practice with it first, so you know it works, how far the range is and how to use it properly. Pepper sprays can have harmful results to you and your pet (if the wind is blowing the wrongs direct). Keep in mind you can make the dog more agitated.

- A horn or a pet compressor can also make at the situation worse: if not used with proper timing, but this can be very effective.

- My personal opinion is that pepper spray is an inhumane correction method to use when you are being attacked and I prefer to carry my taser. It would hurt the dog, but dogs back up when they hear it. Just yell at them, *"no"* and *"stop"*, before they are too close to your dog or you.

What to do When you see a Loose Dog

There are many different levels of dog confrontations. When you first see a loose dog, do not make direct eye contact and keep them in your peripheral vision because a dog could feel threatened and then attack. Do not scream, as it could scare the dog even more.

- Avoid sudden movements. Do not smile, flail your hands, or jump around; especially children.

- Do not walk towards the dog's direction.

- As soon as you see a loose dog, stop and do not run. The dog may run after you or your child because of their instinct to do so. The dog is always going to be faster than you.

- Never turn your back from the dog. It can turn into a charging dog, so always keep your eye on the dog.

- Remain motionless, hands at your sides and avoid direct eye contact with the dog so that you can identify what kind of situation you are in.

Most Common Sign Dogs Give us Before Biting in any Situation

It is important to learn to assess the situation within a few seconds and identify what the dog's body language and behavior are saying; before any potentially dangerous situation gets out of hand.

As soon as the dog hears or sees you coming around the corner, they will be sizing you up. This will take about 3 seconds for you to identify your situation to react and to get them to snap out of it or break out of their *"tunnel vision"*, before they go to bite you. This happens very quickly, so you must always be on alert for you and your dog's safety.

Read the following warning signs:

- Dogs moves a step back, ears are flat back, then they turn their head, like saying that they need space, they may lick their lips (which means that they are in distress), or sniff before they go to bite you.

- Tensed body, a stiff tail, pulled back head and/or ears, furrowed brow, eyes rolled so the whites are visible, yawning, flicking tongue, intense stare or backing away in any situation.

- Signs of aggression. Such as; growling, snarling, baring teeth and lunging are easy to read. There can also be signs that are very subtle. Such as; a moment of tension, a wagging tail (does not always mean their happy to see you. He could be happy to bite you!). Walking back, cowering down, tucked tail, barking and moving toward you.

Growling, crouching, lip biting, tucked tail, snapping, licking lips and lunging toward another dog or backing away are all signs to use extra caution.

If you, even using extra caution, notice a dog has tunnel vision on you or object: he is probably going to attack.

What to do if a dog Is Heading Towards you Aggressively

- Avoid eye contact.

- You must break the tunnel vision.

- Turn your body slowly to the side.

- Cross your arms.

- Completely ignore the dog.

- Be still for a short period, then move slowly away.

- Try to get to a place where there is a barrier between you and the dog.

- Place a board or anything you can find between you and the dog.

- Spray the dog with a water bottle or water hose.

- Bang to make noise on an object or blow an air horn.

- Use the commands, *"no"* and *"stop"*.

- Toss a blanket, towel or your shirt or anything you can find over the top of them.

• Yelling at them will only make the dog react more. Protection

What to do Before a Dog Starts to Attack You!

• If the dog continues to come towards you and makes direct eye contact, do not stand head on with the dog. This can frighten the dog, so just *turn your body at an angle.* With a firm and dominate loud voice say, *"stop",* with your hand in front of you and gesturing with your fingers spread wide apart. *Continue to say, "no" and "stop"*, (every dog should know "no"). If needed, clap your hands and pound your foot firmly on the ground. Repeat as needed. Hopefully, the dogs' owner will hear this and come out or someone else will come to help you when they hear the dog barking.

• **Command your space.**

• **Stay calm** and do not scream. Screaming could easily antagonize the dog more.

• **Once the dog loses interest in you, slowly back away,** until he is out of sight. Keep your eyes on him, until you get yourself out of the situation. Contact your local animal services immediately.

- *Feed the dog your jacket, purse, bicycle or anything that you can put between yourself and the dog for protection. Shield yourself and call for help.* In other word, give them something else to bite and find something to shield yourself.

- **Throw a shirt, towel, blanket or something to *cover his vision*.** Hopefully, this will keep the dog busy so that you can getaway.

If you fall, or are knocked to the ground, which is common, *curl up into a ball* or roll around. Put your hands over your head, cover your face, neck and abdomen area. Remain motionless and try not to scream.   At this point, it could make it worse.

How to Defend Yourself

Dog attacks are a very dangerous situation. Be prepared to defend yourself with some of the safety devices that I mentioned earlier, even if it means unavoidable lethal force. Take cautious measures to protect yourself because it could be the attacking dog or you.

Hitting the dog will only excite the dog even more. Try to act as calmly as possible. If you are witnessing a fight, you can end it by covering the dog's head with a blanket, jacket or shirt. Blocking the dog's vision will normally cause a dog to disengage.

- If you are not prepared, then look for anything to use to defend yourself such as garbage can lids (as a shield), a rake, bag or a shirt. Use anything handy as a barrier or shield between you and the attacking dog. You can get them to bite your purse or backpack instead of you. An umbrella can be used as a weapon or shield. Sometimes opening and closing an umbrella in the dog's face might deter him. Find a nearby car or fence to get behind or climb onto.

- If you have to hit the dog, hit him between the shoulder blades or head.

- Only if you have a clear kick, use everything you have to protect yourself. Be careful that the does not turn around and bite your leg.

- Kick a small dog in the nose. The nose is a very sensitive area and this may deter the dog from biting.

- *If a dog is going to bite you give him your weaker arm,* so that you can use your dominant hand to strike and fight them off. From there, with you needed to protecting yourself (while the dog has a hold on your weaker arm), you have to know where to hit the dog for a release. Go for a sharp strike with everything you have; between the shoulders blade in the spine area, or go under the throat of the dog to cause a vomit reaction.

As difficult as this may be, try not to pull away from the dog that is biting you. *This will only make the dog more aggressive and tear into your skin. Instead, grab the back of their head and press it against your arm.* This way they can not close their mouths (to deepen the injury). Pulling and screaming makes it worse.

How to Stop a Dog From Continuing to Attack a Victim

- **If you can, try aiming the   water hose at the nose**.

- If a dog is attacking the victim, come around to the back of the dog and grab the collar firmly with both hands (if dog does not have collar grab a belt or leash to use as a collar).

- Straddle the dog and immediately squeeze your knees into the dog to immobilize him.

- Twist the collar and then lift it. Squeeze firmly! Wait for the dog to choke a bit, to release their bite.

- Only then should you pull off. If you pull away while the dog is biting, it will cause more damage to victim.

If the dog will not let go, then push the bottom of the dog's neck firmly up to **choke them** and cause the dog to have a vomit reaction and will cause the dog to release the victim.

Always remain calm. It is very dangerous to break up dog fights. It is more **common for the owners to get bitten by their dogs.**

How to Stop a Dog Fight with 2 People

Pull them apart by back legs, lift and move in a circular direction so they do not bite you. Remember that a dog can turn and snap at you. So keep moving in a circle and backward until you get a hold of a dog and to keep them from biting again. Spin fast enough, so the dog doesn't bite again. Lift them up in a wheelbarrow like position. If the dog comes at you at this moment, you may have to slam the dog onto the ground. Get the dogs stretched out, until one of them lets go, or someone else could even put a finger up their butt to get them to let go of the other dog. Yes, that's right, this will snap them out of the attack mode and they will finally let go of the other dog! This is the most effective. Unless the dog is trained for fighting, this can work.

Some people are against this "pull back legs" technique, but it works very well for others. I always grab their legs; from up high, close to stomach up towards from their back side and stomach area of the dog's body so I don't hurt dog's legs. For an older dog, This may be safer to prevent hip injury to the dog.

Stopping a Dog Fight With 1 Person

Always know where at least 2 leashes are. If you are alone and have 2 dogs or more that are fighting; wrap one leash underbelly and thread the latch part through the hand loop. Then wrap around their belly towards the hind legs and pull them up off the ground. If the dogs are still fighting, pull dogs to where you can secure the first dog: hook and latch him. Then try to do the same thing with the other dog. It may take some time for them to settle down, but it will happen.

- Better yet, if you have a special "police leash", you can use this, as it is specially designed for these types of situations. You can easily hook it around their abdomen and back legs. Pull to tighten it and hook the leash to tree or door.

- Stay towards the back area of the dog and do not put your hands around their teeth.
- Use a "dressage whip" (specially designed not to hurt the dog, but it is used as a training) on dogs that will not let go, to snap dog out of their attack mode.

- Break stick: A plastic 10-inch stake, that you can get at any hardware store, can be used a break stick to pop the dog's mouth open. It is risky, but at last resort, you have to use something.

- Look for a proper fit when grabbing the collar to turn the dog's head and inserting it from the side, to keep the dog from being able from biting again. Keep the dog between your legs with a tight hold on the collar to keep control of the dog's neck. Breaks stick can be used to get a dog to let go by first sliding it in the side of the dog's mouth to pry the jaws open. Some

police have used a baton or screwdriver.

• Finger in up butt hole.

What to do if you or Someone Gets Bit by a Dog

Immediately wash the wound thoroughly with soap and warm water.

• Apply pressure and ice immediately to prevent swelling and bruising.

- Contact your physician for additional care and advice. Dogs can bite so hard that it can cause bones to break and they may need an x-ray.

- Report the bite to your local animal care and control agency. Tell the animal control officer everything you can; to avoid issues with other pet owners directly. Animal services will collect all the rabies information on dog for you.

Chapter 11
How to Avoid a Dog Being a
Liability

Dog aggression issues start innocently enough and can be hard to detect if you don't know what signs to look for. It can happen very quickly and you must know what to do; to snap your dog out of the **"tunnel vision"** attack mode. Watch for dominant posture, that can be a "pre-attack" state of mind in a second, and **be able to make the right corrections.** It can make the difference between a good or bad choices for your dog in the future.

Millions of dog owners deal with their dogs having issues within their own homes. This should be worked out with a professional trainer, that specializes in this, to avoid future reoccurrences of any dog attack situations. Also note that older dogs deal with internal pain, social behavior and bringing in a high energy puppy can irritate them and cause them to bite.

You should know that any breed of dog can bite. To prevent liabilities, you should master walking them on a leash as soon as possible. Practicing basic training skills will enable you to properly manage your dogs. What I mean is, by training your dogs the basic commands: *"sit"*, *"lay down"*, *"stay"* and *"come"*, you will be able to take your dog almost anywhere. Make sure first that you have control of your dog and that they are obedient and know that you are the leader of the pack. Often dog owners are overcome by the power of their dog simply by not making early corrections or practicing basic commands while they are young. This can lead to many dangerous situations and issues. When it comes to the life of your pet, never leave anything to chance.

189

Sterilization Spay/Neuter

Spay or neuter your dog, to lessen the risk of aggression problems at a later age. Sterilization is commonly done by the ages of 6-9 months. After 10-12 months, the dog may have already learned aggression. Having testosterone may have developed in their behavior. For a female, the first heat can be a traumatic experience because of badgering by male dogs. The female can develop a learned defensive reaction to being approached by other dogs.

Spaying her later will not change the learned behavior. This also reduces the dog's chances of cancer.

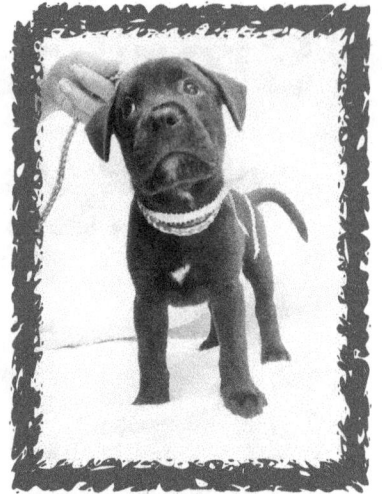

Unfortunately, a study, performed by Dr. Benjamin L. Hart at the University of California, suggests that altered dogs have an increased chance of getting cancers such as; hemanigosarcoma, lymphoma, osteosarcoma, and mast cell tumors (MCT). *The Whole Dog Journal* adds that male dogs who are neutered are also more prone

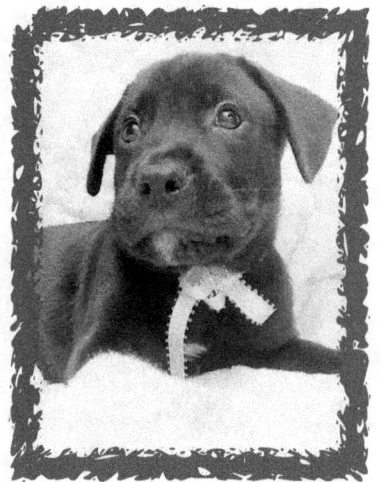

to also developing prostate cancer.

About Your Dog

Introduce your dog at an early age to visitors in your home, community parks, family and friends; even the noise of playing children, busy sidewalks and other animals.

Make sure these experiences are positive and not frightening for them. The more your dog feels safe in a variety of situations, the less chance they will feel compelled to bite. An unsocialized dog can bite because they may feel threatened by new situations and even causing them to run away.

Exercise Your Dog

All dogs need some daily physical exercise. This does not need to exhaust them, but it should make them pleasantly tired. Mental exercise is just as important, so your dog feels like they have had some interesting experiences threw out the course of their day. Bored dogs are more inclined to develop destructive behavior, than dogs whose life is active and interesting for at least an hour or two every day.

Train Your Dogs

It's important to use reward-based methods when training your dog. Only voice reprimands when your dog does something naughty. Do not slap, hit or kick your dog. Don't get angry at mistakes, but instead, try to help the dog understand what you want him or her to do. Provided you choose this kind of training, you can start when the pup is only 7-8 weeks of age. This kind of training can also works well with adult dogs. *The "come" command, is the most important command your dog will ever learn.* A dog who will unhesitatingly come to you when called, can be taken out of a developing, dangerous situation. For example; if you see the dog is becoming frightened or defensive, heading for a busy street, chasing a child, or a cat or getting ready to go greet a dangerous dog.

Constrain Your Dogs

Do not let your dog wander off in your neighborhood. Even if you have a non-aggressive type of
dog. Their experiences while wandering could teach
the dog to be aggressive. Wandering dogs often get

killed by traffic, or can get shot by the police or your neighbors. If you want to have your dog out in the yard, be sure you have a fence that will contain your dog and that will protect them from whatever passes by. It's very common for dogs to get stolen from people's property by strangers. Electric fences may teach dogs to be aggressive to passersby (because the dog gets shocked if they goes to greet them), and they do not protect your dog from dangers that could invade your yard. If a dog leaves an electric-fenced yard in a moment of excitement, they will hesitate to return because returning will mean getting another shock.

Chaining a dog is also not a good idea. Besides, it not being safe, tethering is illegal in most cities. This limits their ability to regulate social space and the

knowledge that they can't flee, if they feel threatened. Feeling safe is important to dogs. If a dog can not get their distance from something is approaching them, they may feel no other choice, but to bite. In some cases, the chained dog may feel they have to desperately defend themselves and develop this behavioral patterns..*A Denver study published in 1994, revealed* that biters were nearly 3 times as likely to be chained as to be unchained. In the past 10-years, many jurisdictions have adopted anti-tethering ordinances as well. Chaining may not even be legal in your city or county.

Limit Exposure to Untested Situations

If your dog is unfamiliar with busy sidewalks, joggers, playgrounds full of screaming children, a room full of unknown guests, them do not expose your dog to these situations, until you know these things that will not frighten your dog. You can gradually train a dog not to fear such situations by socializing them as soon as possible. Simply throwing a dog in at the deep end can lead to a disaster.

If you consider your dog a 'family' dog, understand that the dog may still have to learn that visitors are also welcomed in the house; not just only family members. Do everything you can to teach your dog that humans are trustworthy and not a danger. Make sure all of their experiences with humans are good ones. If in doubt, allow your dog to meet a new guest outdoors and become comfortable with that guest before going indoors together.

When Walking Your Dog

Do not walk a dog too big for you to restrain. You do not have control of a dog if the dog can pull you off your feet or drag you where they want to go. The same caution applies for letting your child hold the leash or walk the dog alone. Do not use a re-

tractable leash, unless it's safe for your dog to lunge the full length of the leash, away from you and for you to have one hand occupied by holding the box part. Many dogs has been run over because a re-tractable leash allows dogs to dash into a street. Many dogs have run in panic when the owner dropped the box, fleeing even further to escape the plastic object that was following it (the box). If the re-tractable leash gets tangled while meeting another dog, this can result in a fight that otherwise would not have taken place.

It's better not to do dog greetings when walking your dog unless you know both dogs are good at greeting on-leash. They know they can't flee if they need to.

Leashed dogs can be defensive when meeting new dogs on-leash. The same goes for letting children greet your pet.

Dog Parks

Many dogs enjoy socializing with their kind at a dog park. However, dogs do not need to have other dog friends to lead a full and happy life. Do not take your dog to a dog park if you can not control them. People always bring dogs with aggression problems to the park and your dog may not know that. Instead, consider play dates with dogs that you do know, and behave normally around other dogs. Do not take your dog to a dog park if you know that your dog has

TANK
RIP

aggression problems. Instead, make sure you do enough interesting things with him during the course of each day, like, walks (dogs need exercise for good for mind and body balance), rides and playing catch! Training with your dog is the best exercise. Your dog will be perfectly happy with this.

Reference research dogsbite.org You can read more about Tank's Story and the truth about shelter dog's lives in my other books that are part of the Everything Dogs Book Collection.

Sterilize, foster, volunteer, donate adopt a shelter or rescue dog!

This is Reba at only 8 months old here, she is pregnant expecting puppies. She was Rescue from Palm Beach County Animal Care & Control by Blessed Paws. Reba Being Rescued Video!

Everything Dogs is a world of dog education and happy dog families!

Good Bye

Thank you for reading my book. I really appreciated you spending time to learn more about dogs and making a difference in their lives.

They mean the world to me! We need to make a difference in animals lives in shelters everywhere, and in every way we can. Let's live in harmony on our journey into the future living along side all animals on this earth.

I wish everyone, happy dog guardianship, knowledge, safety, health, love, many happy memories and harmony on your journey into the future living along side with your furry friends and family members!

Open your heart to fostering, volunteering, donating for more veterinarian medical research, sterilizing, advocating and adopt a shelter dog from your community!

Check out my other dog education books part of the Everything Dogs Series Book Collection

By Mercy Lopez

www.everythingdogs.net

www.ingramcontent.com/pod-product-compliance
Lightning Source LLC
Chambersburg PA
CBHW081537040426
42447CB00014B/3399